Introduction to

Artificial Intelligence,

AI Governance

and

AI Regulations

Second Edition with updates to Legal Frameworks.

Published by Ira Goel

Book and cover design by Ira Goel

ISBN 9798871709382 (Paperback)

ISBN 9798880231805 (Hardback)

Foreword

In "Introduction to Artificial Intelligence, AI Governance and AI Regulations," Ira Goel explores the expansive realm of AI, reflecting her deep insights. Having witnessed Ira's dedication during her time working with me, this book reflects her commitment to demystify the complexities of AI for all.

Embarking on the exploration of AI's essence, the reader is drawn into the significance and multifaceted applications that have become integral to our daily lives. Ira adeptly navigates through the intricacies of AI types and functionalities, shedding light on its diverse capabilities, all while making the subject accessible and engaging.

Moving on, the book delves into AI governance, a theme close to Ira's heart. Her expertise shines through as she articulates the necessity of responsible AI development, emphasizing collaboration and foresight. Readers are guided through the global landscape of AI regulations, a testament to Ira's commitment to fostering an understanding of diverse strategies employed by nations in this transformative era.

In the hands of a seasoned professional like Ira, this book not only educates but also resonates with a personal touch. It is a testament to her tireless dedication to ensuring that the reader, like me, emerges well-equipped to navigate the evolving world of AI with responsibility and foresight. Ira Goel's work remains inspiring, and her book is a valuable resource for anyone looking to understand the impact of AI on our future in a nuanced way.

Nancy Hadley

Preface

Artificial Intelligence (AI) is rapidly transforming how we work, live, and interact with the world. From powering digital services to enhancing public services, AI has become an integral part of our daily lives. However, to fully harness its potential benefits, we must ensure that AI is developed and deployed responsibly.

This book aims to provide readers with a foundational understanding of AI, its governance and the regulatory scene around AI. Whether you're new to the field or seeking to deepen your knowledge, this guide aims to introduce key concepts related to AI assurance and situates them within the broader landscape of AI governance.

Key Topics Covered:

1. AI Assurance: Learn how AI assurance plays a crucial role in building trust. Discover how it provides the basis for consumers to trust that products will work as intended, enables industry innovation while managing risk, and allows regulators to monitor compliance.
2. AI Governance: Understand the frameworks, rules, and standards that direct AI research, development, and application. Explore how governance ensures safety, fairness, and respect for human rights in AI systems.
3. AI Regulations: Dive into the regulatory landscape surrounding AI. Explore proposals for implementing a proportionate, future-proof, and

pro-innovation framework for regulating AI. Additionally, learn about landmark deals such as the European Union's comprehensive laws on regulating AI.

As we navigate this exciting era of technological advancement, let's explore how AI can be harnessed for societal benefit while mitigating risks. Welcome to "Introduction to AI and AI Governance."

Table of Contents

Section: 1 Introduction to Artificial Intelligence

Artificial intelligence (AI) is a term that refers to the ability of machines to perform tasks that normally require human intelligence, such as understanding language, recognizing images, solving problems, and learning from data. AI is not a single technology, but a collection of different methods and tools that can be applied to various domains and challenges.

This section aims to provide a comprehensive and accessible introduction to AI. It will cover the following topics:

Chapter 1: The Dawn of Artificial Intelligence

- Overview of the historical development of artificial intelligence.
- Key milestones and breakthroughs that have shaped the AI landscape.
- Impact of AI on various industries and everyday life.

Chapter 2: Understanding Artificial Intelligence

- Explanation of fundamental AI concepts, including machine learning, deep learning, and neural networks.

Chapter 3: Types of AI and Real-World Applications

- Different types of AI: narrow AI, general AI, and superintelligent AI.
- Real-world applications of AI in fields such as healthcare, finance, transportation, and more.

Chapter 4: Concepts, Technologies and Models of AI

- Different technologies of AI: chatbots, computer vision, neural networks.
- Deep dive in NEL
- Different models: Regressions, decision trees

Chapter 4: The Ethics of AI

- Discussion on the ethical considerations surrounding AI development and deployment.
- Exploration of bias, fairness, accountability, and transparency in AI systems.

Chapter 6: Risks and Challenges in AI

- Examination of potential risks associated with AI, including job displacement, security threats, and unintended consequences.
- Discussion on the challenges of explainability and interpretability in AI systems.
- Overview of current and emerging AI safety measures.

By the end of this section, you will clearly understand what AI is, how it works, and how it can help you in your professional and personal endeavors. You will also have the confidence and curiosity to explore more advanced topics and opportunities in AI.

Chapter 1: The Dawn of Artificial Intelligence

Overview of the Historical Development of Artificial Intelligence

The concept of artificial intelligence (AI) traces its roots back to ancient civilizations, where myths and legends often depicted humanoid beings with lifelike qualities. However, the formal exploration of AI as a scientific discipline began in the mid-20th century.

The term "artificial intelligence" was coined in 1956 during the Dartmouth Conference, a seminal event where early pioneers, including John McCarthy, Marvin Minsky, and others, gathered to discuss the possibilities of creating machines capable of intelligent behavior. This marked the inception of AI as an academic and research field.

Key Milestones and Breakthroughs

Over the decades, AI has experienced significant milestones and breakthroughs that have shaped its trajectory:

1950s- 1960s: The Birth of AI

Early AI research focused on symbolic reasoning, with efforts to create programs that could mimic human thought processes. The development of the Logic Theorist by Allen Newell and Herbert A. Simon in 1955 marked one of the first AI programs capable of problem-solving.

1980s- 1990s: Knowledge-Based Systems and Expert Systems

Knowledge-based systems and expert systems gained prominence, utilizing databases of expert knowledge to make decisions in specific domains. MYCIN, developed in the 1970s, was an early expert system for medical diagnosis.

1997: Deep Blue vs. Kasparov

In a landmark moment, IBM's Deep Blue defeated world chess champion Garry Kasparov in a six-game match, showcasing the power of computing in strategic decision-making.

2011: Rise of Deep Learning

The breakthrough in deep learning, particularly with the advent of deep neural networks, led to significant advancements in image and speech recognition. The ImageNet Large Scale Visual Recognition Challenge in 2012 marked a turning point with the success of deep learning algorithms.

2015: AlphaGo's Triumph

Google's AlphaGo defeated a human Go champion, Lee Sedol, demonstrating the capacity of AI to master complex games with intuition and strategic thinking.

Present: AI in Natural Language Processing and Robotics

Recent years have witnessed tremendous progress in natural language processing, with models like OpenAI's GPT-3 showcasing unprecedented language understanding capabilities. AI-driven robotics have also seen advancements, impacting industries like manufacturing and healthcare.

Impact of AI on Various Industries and Everyday Life

The impact of AI extends across diverse sectors, reshaping industries and influencing everyday experiences:

- Healthcare: AI aids in medical diagnostics, drug discovery, and personalized treatment plans. Machine learning algorithms analyze vast datasets to identify patterns, improving patient outcomes.
- Finance: AI algorithms enhance financial services through fraud detection, algorithmic trading, and personalized financial advice. The technology optimizes decision-making and risk management.
- Manufacturing: AI-driven automation streamlines manufacturing processes, optimizing production efficiency, and quality control. Robotics and machine learning contribute to the evolution of smart factories.
- Education: AI applications facilitate personalized learning experiences, adaptive tutoring, and intelligent assessment tools. Educational technologies powered by AI cater to individual student needs.
- Transportation: Autonomous vehicles leverage AI for navigation and decision-making, transforming the landscape of transportation. AI also optimizes logistics and supply chain management.
- Communication and Entertainment: Natural language processing enables voice-activated assistants, language translation, and sentiment analysis. Content recommendation algorithms in entertainment platforms leverage AI to enhance user experience.

- Everyday Life: AI has become ubiquitous in everyday devices, from virtual assistants on smartphones to smart home systems. Facial recognition, speech synthesis, and predictive text are integral parts of modern technology.

In conclusion, the historical journey of AI from its conceptualization to the present day reflects a continuous quest to replicate and augment human intelligence. Key milestones and breakthroughs have not only shaped the academic landscape but have also permeated various facets of our daily lives, revolutionized industries and contributing to the ongoing evolution of artificial intelligence. This chapter sets the stage for a deeper exploration of the ethical, societal, and regulatory considerations associated with the widespread adoption of AI technologies.

Chapter 2: Understanding Artificial Intelligence

Artificial intelligence (AI) is a term that refers to the ability of machines to perform tasks that normally require human intelligence, such as understanding language, recognizing images, solving problems, and learning from data. AI is not a single technology, but a collection of different methods and tools that can be applied to various domains and challenges.

Artificial intelligence (AI) is the field of computer science that studies and creates systems that can perform tasks that normally require human intelligence, such as reasoning, learning, decision making, and problem solving. AI systems can range from simple programs that play games or recognize faces, to complex systems that drive cars or diagnose diseases. AI systems can also interact with humans and other agents, such as chatbots, robots, or virtual assistants.

AI systems are powered by algorithms, which are sets of rules or instructions that tell the system how to process data and achieve a goal. AI algorithms can be based on different paradigms, such as logic, statistics, neural networks, or evolutionary computation. AI algorithms can also be classified into different types, such as supervised learning, unsupervised learning, reinforcement learning, or deep learning.

AI is a fascinating and rapidly evolving field that has many opportunities and challenges for humanity. AI can enhance our productivity, creativity, and well-being by automating tasks, augmenting our abilities, and providing new insights and solutions. However, AI can also pose ethical, social, legal, and security risks by affecting our privacy, autonomy, accountability, and safety. Therefore, we need to ensure that AI is developed and used in a way that is aligned with our values and interests.

Some of the examples of AI that we encounter in our daily lives are:

- **Google Search**: a web search engine that uses natural language processing and machine learning to provide relevant and personalized results for our queries.
- **Siri**: a virtual assistant that uses natural language processing and speech recognition to understand and respond to our voice commands.
- **Netflix**: a streaming service that uses machine learning and recommendation systems to suggest movies and shows that match our preferences and tastes.
- **Tesla**: a car company that uses computer vision and deep learning to enable autonomous driving and smart features for its vehicles.
- **AlphaGo**: a computer program that uses reinforcement learning and deep neural networks to play the board game Go and defeat human champions.

These are just some examples of AI demonstrating its capabilities and applications in various domains and contexts.

What is AI and why is it important?

AI has become increasingly important in recent years, as it has enabled many innovations and transformations in various aspects of modern life.

For example, AI can help us:

- Communicate more easily and effectively with voice assistants like Siri and Alexa, or chatbots that can have natural conversations.
- Discover new insights and patterns from large and complex data sets, such as customer behavior, market trends, health records or scientific research.
- Optimize business processes and operations, such as supply chain management, inventory control, fraud detection or customer service.
- Enhance our creativity and entertainment, such as generating music, art, videos, or games in the style of our favorite artists or genres.
- Improve our health and well-being by diagnosing diseases, recommending treatments, monitoring vital signs, or providing personalized care.

AI is not only beneficial, but also essential for addressing some of the most pressing challenges and opportunities that we face today and in the future. For instance, AI can help us:

- Combat climate change by reducing greenhouse gas emissions, improving energy efficiency, predicting weather patterns, or developing sustainable solutions.
- Advance scientific discovery by accelerating research, testing hypotheses, simulating experiments, or finding new drugs or materials.
- Promote social good by enhancing education, reducing poverty, improving accessibility, or supporting human rights.
- Ensure security and safety by preventing cyberattacks, detecting threats, protecting privacy, or enforcing laws.

However, AI also poses some risks and challenges that need to be carefully considered and addressed. For example, AI can:

- Cause ethical dilemmas by creating bias, discrimination, unfairness or harm to humans or other living beings.
- Disrupt social norms by changing human behavior, values, culture, or identity.
- Impact employment by replacing human workers, creating new skills gaps, or requiring new forms of education and training.
- Challenge governance by raising legal, regulatory, policy or accountability issues.

Therefore, it is important to develop and use AI in a responsible and trustworthy manner that respects human dignity, rights, and values. This requires collaboration and dialogue among various stakeholders, such as researchers, developers, users, regulators, policymakers, and society at large.

Chapter 3: Types of AI and applications of AI

There are different ways to classify AI systems.

Types of AI Systems based on Criteria

There are different ways to classify AI systems, depending on the criteria used. One common way is to distinguish between narrow AI and general AI based on their capabilities.

Narrow AI (Weak AI):

Narrow AI, also known as weak AI, refers to AI systems designed and trained for a specific task. These systems excel in performing predefined functions but lack the general intelligence and adaptability associated with human cognition. Examples include virtual personal assistants, image recognition systems, and recommendation algorithms.

Characteristics:

- Specialized Functionality: Narrow AI systems are tailored to handle a particular task or set of tasks.
- Limited Scope: They operate within predefined boundaries and lack the ability to adapt or generalize beyond their designed function.
- Examples: Virtual personal assistants like Siri and Alexa, image recognition systems used in facial recognition technology, and recommendation algorithms on streaming platforms.

Applications:

- Task Automation: Narrow AI is widely used for automating specific tasks in various industries, such as data analysis, image processing, and language translation.
- Efficiency Improvement: These systems enhance efficiency and accuracy by focusing on well-defined tasks without the need for broader cognitive abilities.

General AI (Strong AI):

General AI, or strong AI, represents the theoretical concept of AI systems possessing the ability to understand, learn, and apply knowledge across a broad range of tasks at a human-like level. Achieving general AI remains a complex and aspirational goal, and as of now, AI systems are primarily narrow, specialized tools.

Characteristics:

- Adaptability: General AI would possess the capability to adapt to diverse tasks and learn new concepts without explicit programming.
- Human-Like Reasoning: It would exhibit human-like reasoning abilities and understand the context of different situations.
- Versatility: Unlike Narrow AI, General AI could perform a wide array of tasks without specific programming for each task.

Challenges:

- Achieving general AI is an immensely challenging goal, as it requires replicating the complexity and flexibility of the human mind.

- Ethical and safety concerns arise, as the development of highly adaptable and autonomous systems raises questions about control and accountability.

Superintelligent AI:

Superintelligent AI goes beyond human intelligence and capabilities. This speculative concept involves AI systems that surpass human cognitive abilities in every aspect. While superintelligent AI is often discussed in theoretical terms, its realization poses significant ethical and existential concerns.

Characteristics:

- Exponential Cognitive Abilities: Superintelligent AI would exhibit cognitive abilities far beyond the capacity of the human brain.
- Autonomous Learning: These systems could continually self-improve and surpass human intelligence without external intervention.
- Potential for Global Impact: The realization of superintelligent AI raises existential questions and concerns about its impact on society, ethics, and control.

Concerns:

- Ethical Considerations: The development of superintelligent AI raises ethical dilemmas related to control, responsibility, and potential unintended consequences.
- Existential Risks: Speculation about the behavior and impact of superintelligent AI prompts concerns about its potential to reshape the world in ways that may be challenging for humanity to anticipate or control.

While Narrow AI is prevalent in today's applications, the concepts of General AI and Superintelligent AI remain aspirational and theoretical, representing long-term goals and raising important ethical and societal considerations.

Classification Based on Functionality

Another way to classify AI systems is based on their functionalities, or how they operate. Underneath narrow AI, there are four functional categories of AI:

Reactive machines

These are the most basic type of AI systems that can only respond to inputs without any memory or learning. They are designed to perform a single task based on predefined rules or algorithms. An example of a reactive machine is IBM's Deep Blue, which defeated world chess champion Garry Kasparov in 1997.

- **Limited memory machines**: These are AI systems that can store and use some information from past events or experiences to improve their performance or decision making. They can learn from data or feedback, but their memory is short-term and limited. An example of a limited memory machine is a self-driving car, which can use sensor data and previous actions to navigate the road and avoid obstacles.

Theory of mind machines

These are AI systems that can understand and model the mental states, emotions, beliefs, and intentions of other agents, both human and artificial.

They can interact with others in a natural and social way, using language, gestures, or facial expressions. An example of a theory of mind machine is Kismet, a robot developed at MIT that can recognize and express emotions through its eyes, ears, and mouth.

Self-aware machines

These are AI systems that have a sense of self and consciousness. They can reflect on their own actions, goals, and abilities, and modify them accordingly. They can also understand their role and impact in the world. An example of a self-aware machine is Sophia, a humanoid robot developed by Hanson Robotics that can hold conversations, make jokes, and express opinions.

Applications of AI

AI has many applications in various fields and industries, such as healthcare, education, entertainment, finance, security, and more.

Some of the most common and impactful applications of AI that are transforming our world include:

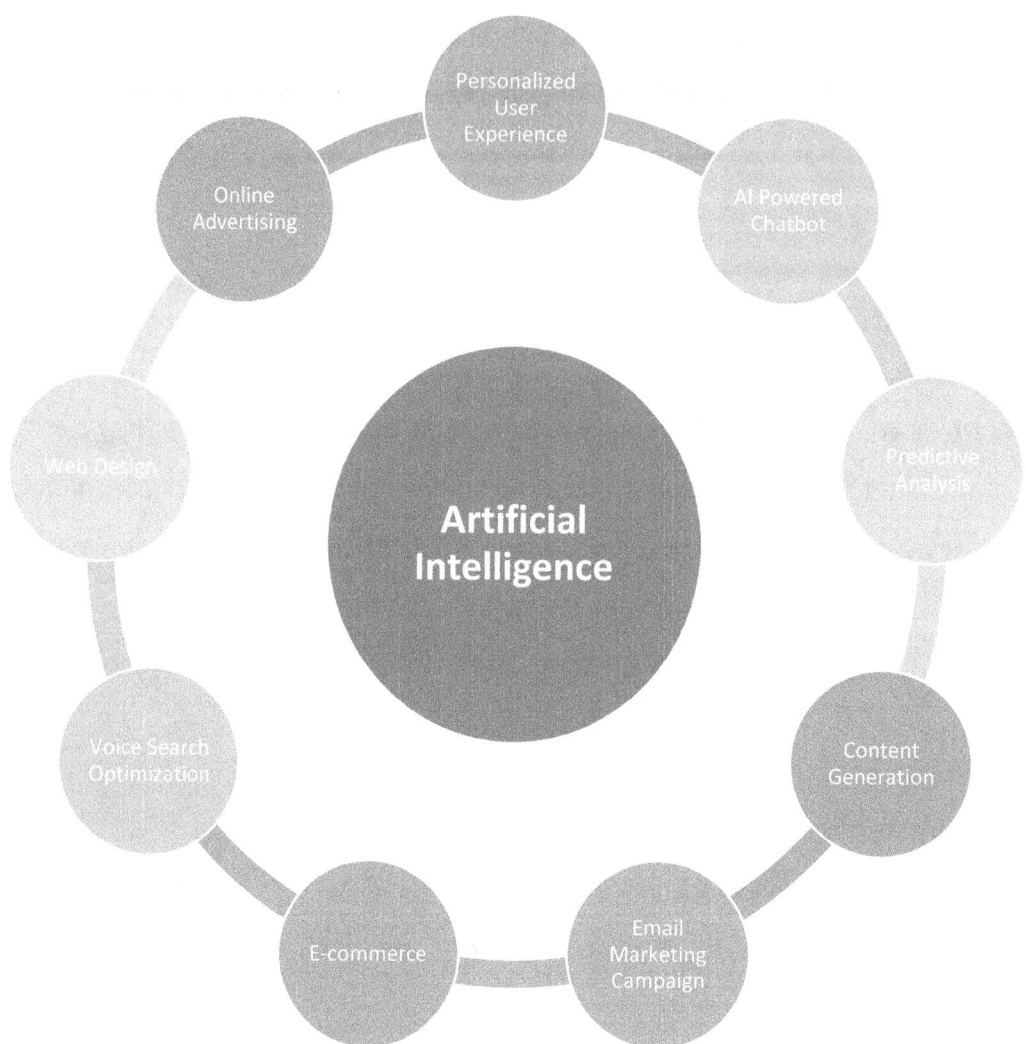

Healthcare

AI is transforming healthcare by facilitating medical diagnostics, personalized treatment plans, and drug discovery. Machine learning algorithms analyze medical data, including imaging and genomics, to improve disease detection and patient outcomes.

Medical Diagnostics:

AI is revolutionizing medical diagnostics by analyzing complex datasets, including medical images, pathology reports, and patient records. Machine learning algorithms can detect patterns indicative of diseases such as cancer, aiding in early and accurate diagnosis.

Personalized Treatment Plans:

AI contributes to personalized medicine by analyzing patient data to tailor treatment plans based on individual characteristics. This includes genetic information, medical history, and lifestyle factors, optimizing the effectiveness of treatments while minimizing side effects.

Drug Discovery:

In drug discovery, AI accelerates the identification of potential therapeutic compounds. Machine learning models analyze vast datasets to predict how molecules interact with biological targets, expediting the drug development process and reducing costs.

Clinical Decision Support Systems:

AI-driven clinical decision support systems assist healthcare professionals in making informed decisions about patient care. These systems analyze patient data, medical literature, and best practices to provide recommendations for diagnosis, treatment plans, and medication choices.

Remote Patient Monitoring:

AI enables remote patient monitoring through wearable devices and sensors. These devices collect real-time data on patients' vital signs, activities, and health metrics. AI algorithms analyze this data to detect trends, predict potential health issues, and alert healthcare providers when intervention is necessary.

Natural Language Processing in Electronic Health Records:
Natural language processing (NLP) is used to extract meaningful insights from unstructured data in electronic health records (EHRs). This facilitates better organization and analysis of patient information, leading to improved patient care, research, and administrative processes.

Robot-Assisted Surgery:
AI plays a role in robot-assisted surgery, enhancing precision and efficiency in complex procedures. Surgeons use robotic systems equipped with AI algorithms for tasks like image analysis, motion planning, and navigation, leading to improved surgical outcomes.

Genomic Analysis:
AI is employed in the analysis of genomic data to identify genetic factors associated with diseases. This information helps in understanding disease risk, developing targeted therapies, and advancing precision medicine initiatives.

Chatbots for Healthcare Support:
AI-powered chatbots provide healthcare support by answering patient queries, scheduling appointments, and offering general health information. These virtual assistants enhance patient engagement and accessibility to healthcare resources.

Epidemiological Forecasting:
AI is utilized in epidemiological forecasting to analyze patterns in health data and predict the spread of diseases. This aids healthcare authorities in planning

interventions, allocating resources, and responding effectively to public health crises.

Finance

In the financial sector, AI plays a crucial role in fraud detection, algorithmic trading, and risk management. Predictive analytics and machine learning models assist in making informed investment decisions and optimizing financial operations.

Fraud Detection:

AI is a powerful tool in identifying fraudulent activities within the financial sector. Machine learning algorithms analyze transaction patterns, detect anomalies, and flag potentially fraudulent transactions in real-time, enhancing security and protecting financial institutions and consumers.

Algorithmic Trading:

AI-driven algorithms enable automated and data-driven trading strategies in financial markets. These algorithms analyze market trends, news, and historical data to execute trades at optimal times, maximizing returns and minimizing risks.

Risk Management:

AI enhances risk management by analyzing vast datasets to identify potential risks and predict market trends. Machine learning models assess credit risks, market fluctuations, and other variables, providing financial institutions with insights to make informed decisions and mitigate potential losses.

Credit Scoring:

AI is employed in credit scoring models to assess the creditworthiness of individuals and businesses. Machine learning algorithms analyze various factors, including financial history, payment behavior, and socio-economic data, to provide more accurate and predictive credit scores.

Customer Service Chatbots:

Financial institutions utilize AI-powered chatbots to provide instant and personalized customer support. These chatbots use natural language processing to understand and respond to customer queries, facilitate account inquiries, and guide users through various financial processes.

Personal Financial Management:

AI-driven personal financial management tools help individuals manage their finances more effectively. These tools analyze spending patterns, provide budgeting recommendations, and offer personalized financial advice to users, empowering them to make informed financial decisions.

Robo-Advisors:

Robo-advisors leverage AI algorithms to provide automated investment advice and portfolio management. These systems analyze user preferences, risk tolerance, and market conditions to create and manage investment portfolios, making financial advisory services more accessible and cost-effective.

Credit Card Fraud Prevention:

AI is employed in credit card fraud prevention by analyzing transaction data and identifying suspicious patterns. Machine learning models can detect unusual spending behavior or transactions that deviate from typical user patterns, helping to prevent unauthorized credit card usage.

Sentiment Analysis:

Financial institutions use sentiment analysis powered by AI to gauge market sentiment from news articles, social media, and other sources. Understanding public sentiment helps investors and financial analysts make more informed decisions about market trends and potential investment opportunities.

Insurance Underwriting:

AI is utilized in insurance underwriting processes to assess risk factors and determine insurance premiums. Machine learning algorithms analyze various data sources, including health records and demographic information, to make more accurate predictions about the likelihood of insurance claims.

Marketing

The transformative impact of AI in the field of marketing is enabling more targeted, personalized, and data-driven approaches. As AI technologies continue to evolve, marketers can harness these capabilities to stay competitive and adapt to changing consumer behaviors.

Customer Segmentation:

In marketing, AI facilitates the segmentation of customer populations based on various criteria such as demographics, behavior, and preferences. This allows businesses to tailor marketing strategies to specific customer segments, improving the effectiveness of campaigns.

Predictive Analytics:

AI-driven predictive analytics analyze historical data and customer behavior to forecast future trends. This enables businesses to anticipate customer needs, optimize inventory management, and make data-driven decisions to enhance overall efficiency.

Chatbots and Virtual Assistants:

AI-powered chatbots and virtual assistants enhance customer interactions by providing real-time support, answering queries, and guiding users through various processes. These applications improve customer service and contribute to a more personalized user experience.

Personalized Content Recommendations:

Content recommendation algorithms powered by AI analyze user behavior and preferences to provide personalized content suggestions. This is widely used in streaming services, e-commerce platforms, and other digital channels, enhancing user experience and increasing engagement.

Dynamic Pricing:

AI enables dynamic pricing strategies by analyzing market conditions, competitor pricing, and customer behavior in real-time. This allows businesses to adjust prices dynamically to optimize revenue, improve competitiveness, and respond to market changes.

Sentiment Analysis:

AI-driven sentiment analysis tools analyze social media, reviews, and other online content to gauge public sentiment about a brand or product. Marketers use this information to understand customer perceptions, identify trends, and shape marketing strategies accordingly.

Email Marketing Optimization:

AI is employed to optimize email marketing campaigns by analyzing user behavior and preferences. This includes personalized content recommendations, optimal send times, and A/B testing to improve open rates, click-through rates, and overall campaign effectiveness.

Visual Recognition and Search:

AI-powered visual recognition systems enhance marketing by enabling image and video analysis. This includes visual search capabilities, where users can search for products using images, and the identification of brand logos and objects in social media content.

Ad Targeting and Optimization:

AI plays a crucial role in ad targeting by analyzing user data to deliver more personalized and relevant advertisements. Advertisers use machine learning algorithms to optimize ad placements, budget allocation, and targeting parameters for better performance.

Marketing Automation:

AI-driven marketing automation platforms streamline repetitive tasks, such as lead scoring, campaign management, and customer segmentation. This allows marketers to focus on strategic decision-making while ensuring consistent and personalized communication with customers.

Manufacturing

AI-driven automation in manufacturing enhances efficiency, quality control, and predictive maintenance. Robotics and machine learning contribute to the evolution of smart factories, optimizing production processes.

Predictive Maintenance:

AI is used in manufacturing for predictive maintenance, where machine learning algorithms analyze equipment sensor data to predict when machinery is likely to fail. This allows for proactive maintenance, reducing downtime and optimizing production efficiency.

Quality Control:

AI-powered image recognition systems are employed in quality control processes. These systems can quickly and accurately identify defects or anomalies in products, ensuring that only high-quality items reach the market.

Supply Chain Optimization:

AI contributes to supply chain optimization by analyzing data from various sources to forecast demand, optimize inventory levels, and enhance overall logistics. This leads to improved efficiency, cost reduction, and increased responsiveness to market changes.

Robotics and Automation:

AI is fundamental to the advancement of robotics and automation in manufacturing. Robots equipped with AI technologies perform tasks such as assembly, welding, and packaging, leading to increased efficiency, precision, and speed in production processes.

Process Optimization:

AI-driven process optimization involves analyzing data from manufacturing processes to identify inefficiencies and opportunities for improvement. Machine learning algorithms can optimize parameters such as temperature, pressure, and speed to enhance overall production efficiency.

Energy Management:

AI is utilized for energy management in manufacturing facilities. Machine learning algorithms analyze energy consumption patterns, optimize usage, and suggest energy-saving measures, contributing to sustainability efforts and cost reduction.

Demand Forecasting:

AI assists in demand forecasting by analyzing historical data, market trends, and external factors. Machine learning models predict future demand, enabling manufacturers to optimize production schedules, reduce excess inventory, and respond to market fluctuations.

Collaborative Robots (Cobots):

Cobots, powered by AI, work alongside human operators in manufacturing environments. These collaborative robots can adapt to changing tasks, improving flexibility and efficiency in production lines. They contribute to a safer and more collaborative working environment.

Customized Production:

AI enables customized production through the analysis of customer preferences and market trends. Machine learning algorithms optimize production processes to accommodate varying product specifications, allowing manufacturers to meet diverse customer demands.

Autonomous Vehicles in Material Handling:

AI-driven autonomous vehicles are used for material handling within manufacturing facilities. These vehicles navigate autonomously, transporting raw materials and finished products efficiently. This reduces manual labor and enhances overall logistics efficiency.

Transportation

Autonomous vehicles leverage AI algorithms for navigation, obstacle detection, and decision-making. AI also optimizes traffic flow, enhances route planning, and contributes to the development of smart transportation systems.

Autonomous Vehicles:

AI plays a pivotal role in the development and operation of autonomous vehicles. Machine learning algorithms process sensor data from cameras, radar, and lidar to navigate through traffic, detect obstacles, and make real-time decisions. This technology is shaping the future of transportation by reducing accidents and improving traffic efficiency.

Traffic Management:

AI optimizes traffic flow in urban areas by analyzing real-time data from cameras, sensors, and GPS devices. Smart traffic management systems use predictive analytics to alleviate congestion, improve signal timings, and enhance overall transportation efficiency.

Route Planning:

AI contributes to efficient route planning by analyzing historical traffic patterns, weather conditions, and real-time data. Navigation apps use machine learning algorithms to provide users with the most optimal routes, considering factors like traffic density and potential delays.

Ride-Sharing and Transportation Platforms:

AI powers ride-sharing platforms by optimizing route planning, matching drivers with riders, and predicting demand. Machine learning algorithms analyze data to enhance the efficiency of transportation networks, reduce waiting times, and improve overall user experiences.

Predictive Maintenance for Vehicles:

AI-driven predictive maintenance analyzes sensor data from vehicles to predict potential mechanical issues and schedule maintenance proactively. This reduces downtime, improves vehicle reliability, and optimizes maintenance costs for transportation fleets.

Smart Parking Solutions:

AI is used to optimize parking solutions by analyzing data on parking availability, pricing, and user preferences. Smart parking systems guide drivers to available parking spaces, reducing congestion and enhancing overall urban mobility.

Public Transportation Optimization:

AI optimizes public transportation systems by analyzing data on ridership, traffic conditions, and scheduling. Machine learning algorithms help improve the efficiency of public transit routes, reducing wait times, and enhancing the overall reliability of transportation services.

Drone Delivery Systems:

AI powers autonomous drone delivery systems for transporting goods. Machine learning algorithms optimize delivery routes, ensure safe navigation, and adapt to changing environmental conditions. Drone delivery systems offer faster and more efficient transportation for small packages.

Traffic Sign Recognition and Interpretation:

AI-based image recognition systems analyze traffic signs and signals. This technology assists vehicles in recognizing and interpreting traffic signs, ensuring adherence to traffic rules and enhancing overall road safety.

Fleet Management and Optimization:

AI contributes to fleet management by analyzing data on vehicle performance, fuel consumption, and maintenance needs. Machine learning algorithms optimize fleet routes, reduce fuel costs, and enhance overall operational efficiency.

Education

AI applications in education include personalized learning platforms, adaptive tutoring systems, and intelligent assessment tools. These technologies cater to individual student needs, providing tailored educational experiences.

Personalized Learning Platforms:

AI-powered personalized learning platforms adapt educational content based on individual student progress, preferences, and learning styles. These platforms provide customized lessons, quizzes, and assessments to cater to each student's unique needs, fostering a more effective and personalized learning experience.

Adaptive Tutoring Systems:

AI-driven adaptive tutoring systems assess students' strengths and weaknesses, tailoring instructional content to address specific areas of improvement. These systems use machine learning to dynamically adjust the difficulty level of questions and exercises, ensuring an adaptive and engaging learning journey.

Intelligent Assessment Tools:

AI facilitates the development of intelligent assessment tools that can automatically evaluate student performance. These tools use natural language processing and machine learning to grade assignments, provide feedback, and assist educators in gauging individual and overall class progress.

Virtual Classrooms and Online Learning:

AI contributes to the development of virtual classrooms and online learning environments. Machine learning algorithms can personalize the online learning experience, track student engagement, and provide real-time feedback to educators for more effective remote education.

Automated Administrative Tasks:

AI is used to automate administrative tasks in educational institutions. This includes tasks such as grading, scheduling, and managing student records. Automation of routine administrative processes allows educators to focus more on teaching and mentoring students.

Smart Content Recommendation Systems:

Content recommendation systems powered by AI analyze students' learning history and preferences to suggest relevant educational materials. This includes recommended readings, videos, and interactive resources tailored to individual student needs.

Language Learning Apps:

AI-driven language learning apps utilize natural language processing and speech recognition to provide personalized language learning experiences.

These apps adapt to individual proficiency levels, offering customized lessons and practice exercises.

Early Intervention Systems:

AI is employed in early intervention systems to identify students who may be at risk of falling behind. Machine learning algorithms analyze academic performance and behavior patterns to provide timely interventions, allowing educators to address potential challenges proactively.

Automated Grading Systems:

AI is used in automated grading systems to evaluate multiple-choice, short-answer, and essay questions. Machine learning models can assess written responses, providing faster and more consistent grading while allowing educators to focus on qualitative feedback.

Learning Analytics:

Learning analytics powered by AI analyze data on student performance, engagement, and interactions with educational content. This information helps educators gain insights into learning patterns, identify areas for improvement, and tailor teaching strategies to enhance overall learning outcomes.

Customer Service

Chatbots and virtual assistants powered by AI enhance customer service experiences. Natural language processing enables these systems to understand and respond to user queries, providing quick and efficient support.

Chatbots and Virtual Assistants:

AI-powered chatbots and virtual assistants enhance customer service across various industries. These systems use natural language processing to understand and respond to customer queries, provide information, and assist with problem resolution. They offer 24/7 support, improving accessibility and efficiency in customer interactions.

Sentiment Analysis:

AI algorithms perform sentiment analysis on customer interactions, analyzing text, voice, or social media inputs to gauge customer satisfaction. This information helps businesses identify areas for improvement, enhance customer experiences, and address issues proactively.

Automated Call Centers:

AI is utilized in automated call centers to handle routine customer inquiries and tasks. Interactive voice response (IVR) systems powered by AI can understand and respond to spoken language, providing a more efficient and streamlined customer service experience.

Personalized Recommendations:

AI is employed to provide personalized product and service recommendations based on customer preferences and past behavior. This enhances the customer experience by offering tailored suggestions, increasing customer satisfaction, and driving sales.

Predictive Customer Service:

AI contributes to predictive customer service by analyzing data to anticipate customer needs and potential issues. Machine learning models can predict customer behavior, enabling businesses to address concerns before they escalate and proactively offer solutions.

Social Media Monitoring and Engagement:

AI tools monitor social media platforms for customer mentions, reviews, and comments. This allows businesses to engage with customers in real-time, address concerns, and participate in relevant conversations, enhancing brand perception and customer satisfaction.

Email Automation:

AI is used for email automation in customer service, allowing businesses to respond to customer inquiries, process orders, and provide information automatically. This improves response times, reduces manual workload, and ensures consistent communication.

Virtual Customer Service Agents:

AI-driven virtual customer service agents handle customer queries and provide support through various channels. These agents can understand natural language, process information, and offer solutions, providing a seamless and efficient customer service experience.

Customer Feedback Analysis:

AI tools analyze customer feedback from various sources, such as surveys, reviews, and online forums. This helps businesses gain insights into customer preferences, identify areas for improvement, and make data-driven decisions to enhance the overall customer experience.

Dynamic FAQs and Knowledge Bases:

AI-powered dynamic FAQs and knowledge bases continually learn from customer interactions to provide accurate and relevant information. This ensures that customers can easily find answers to their queries, reducing the need for human intervention in routine support issues.

Entertainment

Content recommendation algorithms powered by AI enhance user experiences in entertainment platforms. AI technologies enable personalized content suggestions, voice-activated interfaces, and immersive gaming experiences.

Content Recommendation Algorithms:

AI-driven content recommendation algorithms are prevalent in entertainment platforms, such as streaming services. These algorithms analyze user preferences, viewing history, and behavior to suggest personalized content, enhancing user engagement and satisfaction.

Voice-Activated Interfaces:

Voice-activated interfaces, powered by AI technologies like natural language processing, enable users to interact with entertainment devices using voice commands. This includes voice-controlled smart speakers, virtual assistants, and gaming systems, providing a more intuitive and hands-free user experience.

Immersive Gaming Experiences:

AI enhances gaming experiences by enabling realistic simulations, dynamic storytelling, and adaptive gameplay. Machine learning algorithms can create non-player characters (NPCs) with human-like behavior, generate unique storylines, and adapt game difficulty based on player performance, contributing to immersive and engaging gaming experiences.

Virtual Reality (VR) and Augmented Reality (AR):

AI contributes to immersive experiences in virtual and augmented reality applications. AI algorithms enhance spatial awareness, object recognition, and interaction within virtual environments, creating more realistic and engaging simulations.

Personalized Content Creation:

AI is used in personalized content creation, such as generating music playlists, suggesting video edits, and creating personalized news feeds. These algorithms analyze user preferences to curate content that aligns with individual tastes.

Predictive Analytics for Audience Engagement:

AI-driven predictive analytics analyze data to predict audience engagement and preferences. This information helps content creators and broadcasters tailor their offerings to better align with audience expectations, enhancing overall viewer satisfaction.

Content Moderation:

AI is employed for content moderation on platforms to identify and filter inappropriate or offensive content. Machine learning algorithms analyze text, images, and videos to ensure a safer and more enjoyable online environment for users.

Automated Video Editing:

AI is used for automated video editing to enhance post-production processes. Machine learning algorithms can analyze video content, identify key moments, and automatically generate edited versions, saving time and effort for content creators.

Interactive Storytelling:

AI contributes to interactive storytelling experiences by adapting narratives based on user choices. This is used in interactive films, games, and virtual experiences, allowing users to shape the direction of the story.

Music and Lyrics Generation:

AI technologies generate music and lyrics by analyzing patterns in existing compositions. This is used to create original compositions or assist musicians and composers in the creative process.

These real-world applications demonstrate the versatile and transformative impact of AI across diverse sectors, enhancing efficiency, personalization, and overall user experiences. As AI technologies continue to evolve, their integration into various industries is likely to expand, unlocking new possibilities for innovation and advancement.

In summary, understanding the fundamental concepts of AI, differentiating between types of AI, and recognizing real-world applications are crucial steps in comprehending the impact of AI on various industries. As we delve deeper into AI governance and ethical considerations, this foundational knowledge sets the stage for evaluating the responsible development and deployment of AI technologies.

Chapter 4: Concepts, Technologies, and Models of AI

In this chapter, we will embark on a comprehensive exploration of the fundamental elements that constitute the field of AI. From Machine Learning (ML) to cutting-edge models like GPT-3, we will unravel the intricacies that make AI a dynamic and transformative discipline.

Chatbots: These are AI systems that can simulate natural conversations with human users through text or voice. They can provide customer service, information, guidance, or entertainment in real time. An example of a chatbot is ChatGPT, which uses large language models to generate text in response to questions or comments posed to it.

Speech Recognition: One of the most popular applications of AI is speech recognition, which enables machines to understand and process human speech. Speech recognition can be used for voice assistants, such as Siri, Alexa, and Google Assistant, that can answer questions, control smart devices, play music, and more. Speech recognition can also be used for transcription, translation, captioning, and dictation services, such as Google Translate, YouTube, and Microsoft Word.

Computer Vision: This is the field of AI that deals with enabling machines to see and understand visual information, such as images or videos. It involves tasks such as object detection, face recognition, scene understanding, optical character recognition (OCR), and more. Computer vision can be used for face recognition, which can unlock smartphones, verify identities, and tag photos. Computer vision can also be used for object detection, which can identify and locate objects in a scene, such as cars, pedestrians, animals, and more. Object detection can be useful for autonomous vehicles, security cameras, wildlife conservation, and more. An example of computer vision is Google Photos, which can automatically organize, label, and search your photos based on their content.

Natural language processing (NLP): This is the field of AI that deals with enabling machines to understand and generate natural language, such as speech or text. NLP can be used for text summarization, which can condense long documents into shorter summaries. NLP can also be used for sentiment analysis, which can detect the emotions and opinions expressed in texts. Sentiment analysis can be helpful for customer feedback, social media analysis, product reviews, and more.

Machine Learning (ML): ML enables machines to learn from data and improve their performance without explicit programming. ML can be used for recommendation systems, which can suggest products, services, or content based on user preferences and behavior. ML can also be used for anomaly detection, which can spot unusual or suspicious patterns in data. Anomaly detection can be beneficial for fraud detection, cybersecurity, health monitoring, and more.

To explore these ideas further, let's examine them more closely.

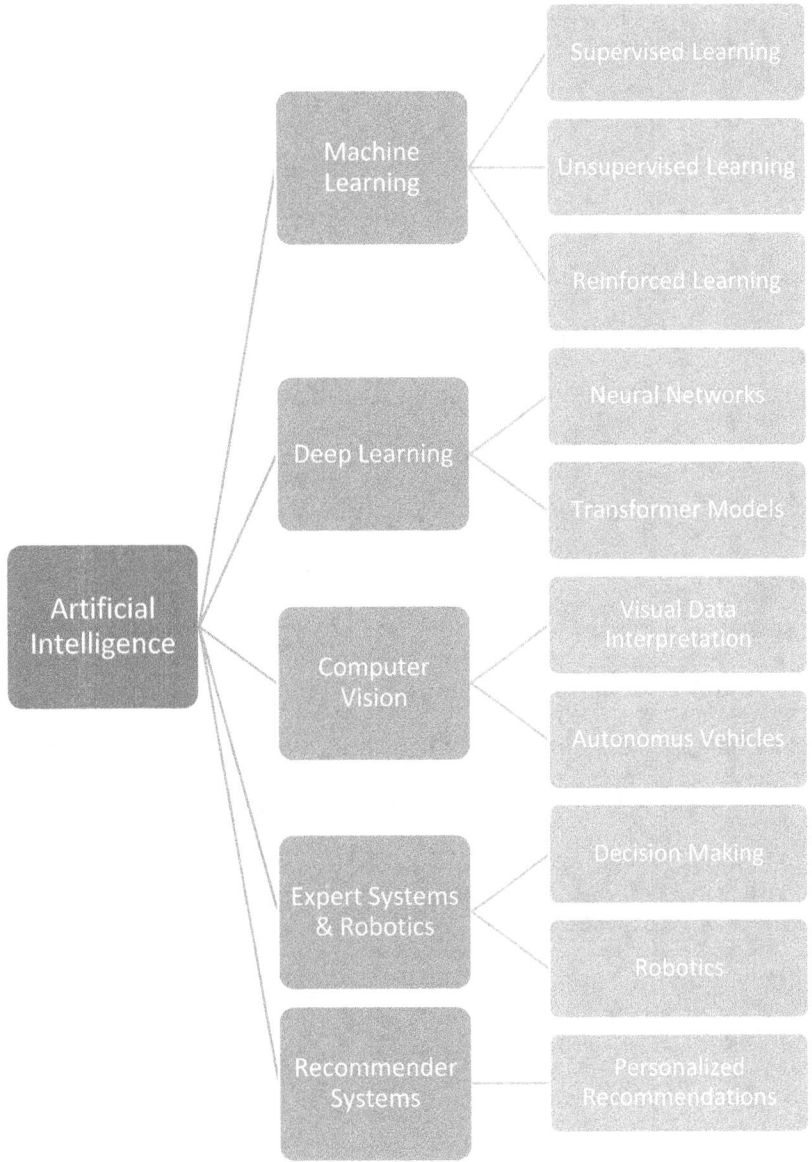

Machine Learning

Machine learning (ML) is the branch of AI that focuses on creating systems that can learn from data and improve their performance without explicit programming. ML algorithms can be divided into three main types: supervised learning, unsupervised learning, and reinforcement learning.

1. Supervised learning is the process of learning a function that maps inputs to outputs based on labeled data, such as images with captions or texts with sentiments. For example, a supervised learning algorithm can learn to classify images of cats and dogs based on their features, such as fur color, shape, size, etc.

2. Unsupervised learning is the process of discovering patterns and structures in unlabeled data, such as clustering similar documents or generating realistic images. For example, an unsupervised learning algorithm can learn to group news articles based on their topics, such as sports, politics, entertainment, etc., or generate new images of faces that do not exist in the real world.

3. Reinforcement learning is the process of learning how to act in an environment by trial and error, based on rewards and penalties, such as playing a game or controlling a robot. For example, a reinforcement learning algorithm can learn to play chess by playing against itself or other opponents, and improving its strategy based on the outcome of each move.

Deep Learning

Deep learning (DL) is a subset of ML that uses multiple layers of artificial neural networks to learn complex and nonlinear functions from large amounts of data.

- Neural networks are composed of interconnected units called neurons that can perform simple mathematical operations on their inputs and pass them to the next layer. DL can achieve state-of-the-art results in many tasks, such as image recognition, natural language processing, speech recognition, etc., by using various architectures and techniques, such as convolutional neural networks, recurrent neural networks, attention mechanisms, transformers, etc.

- Convolutional neural networks (CNNs) are a type of neural network that use convolutional layers to extract features from images or other types of data that have a spatial structure. For example, CNN can learn to recognize faces by applying filters that detect edges, shapes, colors, etc., at different levels of abstraction.

- Recurrent neural networks (RNNs) are a type of neural network that use recurrent layers to process sequential data, such as text or speech. For example, an RNN can learn to generate sentences by predicting the next word based on the previous words.

- Attention mechanisms are a technique that allow neural networks to focus on the most relevant parts of the input or output data. For example, an attention mechanism can help a neural network to translate a sentence by aligning each word in the source language with the corresponding word in the target language.

- Transformers are a type of neural network that use attention mechanisms to encode and decode sequential data without using recurrent layers. For example, a transformer can learn to summarize a text by encoding its meaning into a fixed-length vector and decoding it into a shorter text.

NLP

Natural language processing (NLP) is the branch of AI that deals with the analysis and generation of natural language, such as text or speech. NLP involves many tasks, such as parsing, sentiment analysis, machine translation, summarization, question answering, dialogue systems, etc. NLP relies on various methods and tools, such as linguistic rules, statistical models, neural networks, word embeddings, etc., to process and understand natural language at different levels, such as morphology, syntax, semantics, pragmatics, etc.

- Parsing is the task of analyzing the grammatical structure of a sentence, such as identifying its parts of speech, phrases, clauses, etc. For example, a parsing algorithm can determine that "The cat chased the mouse" is composed of a noun phrase ("The cat"), a verb phrase ("chased"), and another noun phrase ("the mouse").

- Sentiment analysis is the task of detecting the emotional tone or attitude of a text, such as positive, negative, neutral, angry, happy, etc. For example, a sentiment analysis algorithm can determine that "I love this movie" is positive, while "I hate this movie" is negative.

- Machine translation is the task of converting a text from one language to another, such as from English to German or vice versa. For example, a machine translation algorithm can translate "Hello world" to "Hallo Welt" or "Guten Tag Welt".

- Summarization is the task of producing a concise and informative summary of a longer text, such as an article, a book, or a speech. For example, a summarization algorithm can generate a summary of this book by selecting the most important sentences or keywords.

- Question answering is the task of providing a direct and accurate answer to a natural language question, such as "Who is the president of Germany?" or "What is the capital of Germany?". For example, a question answering algorithm can answer these questions by extracting the relevant information from a knowledge base or a document.
- Dialogue systems are systems that can engage in natural language conversations with humans or other agents, such as chatbots, personal assistants, or customer service agents. For example, a dialogue system can chat with a user about their preferences, recommend products or services, or provide information or assistance.

Computer Vision

Computer vision (CV) is the branch of AI that deals with the understanding and manipulation of visual information, such as images or videos. It involves many tasks, such as face detection, object recognition, scene segmentation, optical character recognition, face recognition, image synthesis, etc.

CV relies on various methods and tools, such as feature extraction, edge detection, template matching, machine learning, deep learning, etc., to analyze and interpret visual information at different levels, such as pixels, regions, objects, scenes, etc.

- Face detection is the task of locating and bounding the faces of humans or other animals in an image or a video. For example, a face detection algorithm can draw a rectangle around each face in a group photo.

- Object recognition is the task of identifying and classifying the objects in an image or a video, such as cars, dogs, flowers, etc. For example, an object recognition algorithm can label each object in an image with its name and category. Scene segmentation is the task of dividing an image or a video into meaningful regions that correspond to different parts of the scene, such as sky, ground, buildings, etc. For example, a scene segmentation algorithm can color each region in an image with a different color.

- Optical character recognition (OCR) is the task of converting images of text into editable and searchable text. For example, an OCR algorithm can extract the text from a scanned document or a signboard. Face recognition is the task of verifying or identifying the identity of a person based on their face. For example, a face recognition algorithm can unlock a smartphone or grant access to a building by comparing the face of the user with a stored face template. Image synthesis is the task of generating new images that are realistic and diverse. For example, an image synthesis algorithm can create new images of faces that do not exist in the real world or modify existing images by changing their attributes, such as age, gender, expression, etc.

More about NLP

NLP is a challenging and fascinating field because natural language is rich, complex, and ambiguous. Natural language can have multiple meanings, depending on the context, the speaker, the listener, the culture, the intention, etc. For example, the word "bank" can mean a financial institution, a river shore, or a verb meaning to tilt or turn. The sentence "I saw her duck" can mean that I observed her pet bird, that I witnessed her bending down, or that I used a saw to cut her duck. The phrase "Let's eat grandma" can mean that we are inviting our grandmother to join us for a meal, or that we are planning to cannibalize her.

To deal with these challenges, NLP systems need to perform various subtasks, such as:

- **Tokenization**: splitting a text into smaller units, such as words or characters. For example, the sentence "I love NLP" can be tokenized into three words: "I", "love", and "NLP".
- **Lemmatization**: reducing words to their base or dictionary form, such as verbs to their infinitive or nouns to their singular form. For example, the words "loves", "loved", and "loving" can be lemmatized to "love".
- **Stemming**: removing the affixes from words to obtain their root form, such as prefixes or suffixes. For example, the words "running", "runner", and "runnable" can be stemmed to "run".
- **Part-of-speech tagging**: assigning a grammatical category to each word in a text, such as noun, verb, adjective, etc. For example, in the sentence "She runs fast", the word "she" is a pronoun, the word "runs" is a verb, and the word "fast" is an adverb.
- **Parsing**: analyzing the syntactic structure of a sentence, such as identifying its phrases, clauses, and dependencies. For example, in the sentence "She gave him a book", the word "she" is the subject of the verb "gave", the word "him" is the indirect object of the verb "gave", and the word "a book" is the direct object of the verb "gave".

- **Named entity recognition**: identifying and classifying the proper names of persons, organizations, locations, dates, etc., in a text. For example, in the sentence "Barack Obama was born in Hawaii on August 4th 1961", the word "Barack Obama" is a person name entity, the word "Hawaii" is a location name entity, and the phrase "August 4th 1961" is a date name entity.

- **Sentiment analysis**: detecting the emotional tone or attitude of a text, such as positive, negative, neutral, angry, happy, etc. For example, the sentence "I love NLP" has a positive sentiment, while the sentence "I hate NLP" has a negative sentiment.

- **Machine translation**: converting a text from one language to another, such as from English to German or vice versa. For example, the sentence "I love NLP" can be translated to "Ich liebe NLP" in German or "Me encanta NLP" in Spanish.

- **Summarization**: producing a concise and informative summary of a longer text, such as an article, a book, or a speech. For example, a summarization system can generate a summary of this book by selecting the most important sentences or keywords.

- **Question answering**: providing a direct and accurate answer to a natural language question, such as "Who is the president of Germany?" or "What is the capital of Germany?". For example, a question answering system can answer these questions by extracting the relevant information from a knowledge base or a document.

- **Dialogue systems**: systems that can engage in natural language conversations with humans or other agents, such as chatbots, personal assistants, or customer service agents. For example, a dialogue system can chat with a user about their preferences, recommend products or services, or provide information or assistance.

NLP is also a rapidly evolving field that benefits from the advances in deep learning, big data, cloud computing and other technologies. NLP researchers and practitioners are constantly developing new methods, models, and tools to tackle new problems and improve existing solutions. NLP is becoming more accessible and ubiquitous thanks to the availability of open-source frameworks, libraries, and datasets.

One of the most intriguing questions in NLP is what is the future of this field? How will NLP impact our lives and society in the coming years? What are the opportunities and challenges that lie ahead?

Ethical Implications of NLP

NLP applications have the potential to bring many benefits to individuals and society, such as enhancing communication, education, entertainment, health care, business and more. However, they also pose some ethical risks and challenges that need to be addressed carefully. Some of these issues include:

- **Privacy**: NLP applications often require access to large amounts of personal or sensitive data, such as emails, messages, social media posts, voice recordings and more. How can we ensure that this data is collected, stored, and processed in a secure and respectful way? How

can we protect the privacy rights of the data owners and users? How
can we prevent unauthorized or malicious use of this data?

- **Bias**: NLP applications often rely on data that may reflect human biases
  or prejudices, such as racism, sexism, ageism and more. How can we
  ensure that these biases are not amplified or reproduced by the NLP
  systems? How can we detect and mitigate bias in NLP models and
  outputs? How can we promote fairness and diversity in NLP
  applications?

- **Accountability**: NLP applications often involve complex and opaque
  algorithms that may produce unexpected or erroneous results. How
  can we ensure that these results are accurate and reliable? How can
  we explain how the NLP systems work and why they produce certain
  outputs? How can we assign responsibility and liability for the
  outcomes of NLP applications?

- **Social impact**: NLP applications may have significant social impact on
  individuals and groups, such as influencing their opinions, emotions,
  behaviors, and relationships. How can we ensure that these impacts
  are positive and beneficial? How can we prevent or minimize negative
  or harmful impacts? How can we respect the values and preferences of
  different users and stakeholders?

These are some of the ethical questions that need to be considered when
developing or using NLP applications. There is no simple or universal answer to
these questions. They require careful analysis and deliberation from multiple
perspectives and disciplines. They also require collaboration and dialogue
among researchers, developers, users, policy makers and other stakeholders.

We believe that ethical awareness and responsibility are essential for advancing NLP research and practice in a sustainable and human-centric way.

AI Models

AI models are programs that can recognize patterns or make decisions based on data and algorithms. AI modeling techniques are the methods and tools used to create and train AI models. There are different types of AI models and modeling techniques, depending on the complexity, architecture, and purpose of the model.

Some of the common types of AI models are:

- **Linear regression**: a model that predicts a continuous output variable based on one or more input variables, using a linear function.

- **Logistic regression**: a model that predicts a binary output variable based on one or more input variables, using a logistic function.

- **Decision trees**: a model that predicts an output variable based on a series of rules or conditions, using a tree-like structure.

- **Neural networks**: a model that mimics the structure and function of biological neurons, using layers of interconnected nodes that process and transmit information.

- **Deep learning**: a model that uses multiple layers of neural networks to learn complex and abstract features from large and high-dimensional data.

Chapter 5: Ethics in AI

Artificial intelligence (AI) has the potential to bring about significant benefits to society, but its development and deployment raise complex ethical considerations. This chapter delves into the ethical dimensions of AI, exploring issues such as bias, fairness, accountability, and transparency. Through case studies, we examine real-world examples of ethical challenges in AI and their consequences.

Ethical Considerations Surrounding AI Development and Deployment

AI technologies wield considerable power and influence over various aspects of human life, from healthcare and finance to criminal justice and social media. Consequently, ethical considerations are paramount in guiding the responsible development and deployment of AI systems. Key ethical principles that inform discussions on AI ethics include:

Respect for Human Autonomy:

AI systems should respect individuals' autonomy and agency, ensuring that decisions made by AI do not unduly infringe upon human rights or freedoms.

Beneficence and Non-Maleficence:

AI developers and practitioners have a responsibility to maximize the benefits of AI while minimizing harm to individuals and society at large.

Justice and Fairness:

AI systems should be designed and implemented in a manner that promotes fairness and equity, avoiding discrimination or bias against any particular group.

Transparency and Accountability:

There should be transparency in how AI systems operate, with clear mechanisms for accountability and recourse in cases of errors or misuse.

Ethical Principles

The ethical considerations in AI revolve around fundamental principles that guide its responsible use. These principles include transparency, fairness, accountability, privacy, and ensuring that AI systems align with human values. Striking a balance between innovation and ethical considerations is crucial for the sustainable and beneficial integration of AI into society.

1. Bias in AI:

   One of the primary ethical concerns is the presence of bias in AI systems. Bias can emerge from training data that reflects historical inequalities or human prejudices. Understanding and mitigating bias in AI algorithms is essential to prevent discriminatory outcomes and promote fairness in decision-making processes.

2. Fairness and Accountability:

Ensuring fairness in AI systems requires careful consideration of how algorithms impact different groups. Accountability is another crucial aspect, necessitating clarity on who is responsible for the decisions made by AI systems. Establishing accountability mechanisms becomes challenging as AI systems become more complex and autonomous.

3. Transparency:

Transparency in AI refers to the openness and clarity surrounding how AI systems operate. The "black box" nature of some advanced AI algorithms poses challenges, as it can be difficult to understand the decision-making processes. Striving for transparency helps build trust and allows users to comprehend and challenge AI-driven decisions.

Bias in AI

Although beneficial, AI comes with challenges, especially bias in different forms because of human beings who design, develop and train AI for its designed purpose. Some of the different kinds of bias in AI and how they can affect various domains and applications.

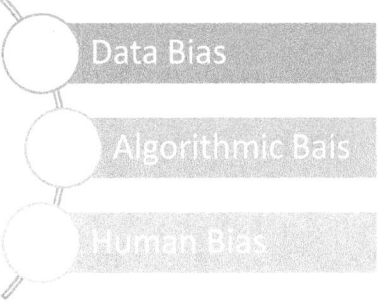

Data bias

Data bias refers to the situation where the data used to train or test an AI system is not representative of the real-world population or scenario that the system is intended to serve. Data bias can result from various factors, such as:

- **Implicit bias**: This is when the data reflects the unconscious or hidden assumptions, preferences, or prejudices of the data collectors, annotators, or users. For example, an AI system that analyzes job applications may inherit the implicit bias of human recruiters who favor certain names, genders, or ethnicities over others.

- **Sampling bias**: This is when the data is not collected or selected in a random or balanced way, leading to over- or underrepresentation of certain groups or features. For example, an AI system that performs facial recognition may have sampling bias if the data contains more images of white people than people of color, resulting in lower accuracy for the latter group.

- **Temporal bias**: This is when the data becomes outdated or irrelevant due to changes in the environment, behavior, or preferences over time. For example, an AI system that recommends products or services may have temporal bias if the data does not reflect the current trends, needs, or tastes of the customers.

- **Overfitting**: This is when the AI system learns too much from the data and becomes too specific or complex for the problem at hand, leading to poor generalization or adaptation to new or unseen data. For example, an AI system that detects spam emails may overfit if it learns from a limited or noisy data set that contains many false positives or negatives, resulting in high error rates for new emails.

Algorithm bias

Algorithm bias refers to the situation where the algorithm or model used to process or analyze the data produces biased results due to its design, implementation, or optimization. Algorithm bias can result from various factors, such as:

- **Selection bias**: This is when the algorithm or model is chosen based on convenience, availability, or popularity rather than suitability, performance, or fairness. For example, an AI system that predicts credit scores may have selection bias if it uses a linear regression model that does not capture the nonlinear relationships between the variables.

- **Confirmation bias**: This is when the algorithm or model is tuned or validated based on pre-existing beliefs, expectations, or hypotheses rather than objective evidence or criteria. For example, an AI system that diagnoses diseases may have confirmation bias if it uses a training set that confirms the diagnoses of human doctors rather than independent tests.

- **Measurement bias**: This is when the algorithm or model uses inaccurate, incomplete, or inappropriate metrics or indicators to evaluate its results or performance. For example, an AI system that generates captions for images may have measurement bias if it uses a metric that only measures word overlap rather than semantic meaning.

- **Optimization bias**: This is when the algorithm or model optimizes for a single objective or criterion without considering other relevant factors or trade-offs. For example, an AI system that allocates resources may have optimization bias if it maximizes efficiency without accounting for equity, diversity, or sustainability.

Human bias

Human bias refers to the situation where the human decisions involved in developing and deploying AI systems introduce or amplify bias in the systems. Human bias can result from various factors, such as:

- **Framing bias**: This is when the problem definition, scope, or context influences how the data is collected, analyzed, or interpreted. For example,

Exploration of Bias, Fairness, Accountability, and Transparency in AI Systems

Bias:

Bias in AI systems arises from the data used to train them, as well as the algorithms and decision-making processes employed. Biased AI can perpetuate and exacerbate existing inequalities, leading to discriminatory outcomes, particularly in areas such as hiring, lending, and criminal justice.

Exploration:

- Data Bias: Bias often originates from historical inequalities and biases present in training data. If the training data is not diverse and representative, the AI system may replicate and perpetuate existing biases.

- Algorithmic Bias: The algorithms themselves can introduce bias due to their design and training process. Developers must be vigilant in identifying and mitigating bias in the algorithms to ensure fair and equitable outcomes.
- Impact on Decision-Making: Bias in AI can lead to discriminatory outcomes, affecting individuals or groups unfairly. This is particularly concerning in applications like hiring, lending, and criminal justice, where biased decisions can have profound real-world consequences.

Fairness:

Ensuring fairness in AI systems involves mitigating bias and ensuring equitable treatment for all individuals, regardless of race, gender, or other demographic factors. Fairness metrics and algorithms are being developed to assess and address fairness concerns in AI.

The inherent biases present in training data can lead to biased outcomes in AI systems. For instance, facial recognition algorithms may exhibit racial bias, impacting minority groups disproportionately. Addressing bias requires diverse and representative datasets, as well as ongoing monitoring and adjustments to algorithms.

Exploration:

- Algorithmic Fairness: Ensuring fairness in algorithms requires considering the impact on different demographic groups. Developers must implement measures to detect and mitigate biases, striving for equal treatment across diverse populations.

- Group and Individual Fairness: Fairness considerations extend to both groups and individuals. AI systems should not disproportionately favor or harm specific groups, and decisions should be fair to individuals regardless of their characteristics.
- Mitigating Unintended Consequences: Developers need to anticipate and address unintended consequences of AI applications, especially those that may disproportionately impact marginalized or vulnerable communities.

Accountability:

AI systems must be held accountable for their actions and decisions. However, the opaque nature of many AI algorithms poses challenges to accountability. Establishing clear lines of responsibility and accountability is essential to address issues of liability and ensure recourse for individuals affected by AI decisions.

As AI systems become more autonomous, establishing accountability becomes complex. The lack of direct human involvement in decision-making raises questions about responsibility. Legal and ethical frameworks need to evolve to clearly define accountability, ensuring that developers, users, and organizations are accountable for the actions of AI systems.

Exploration:

- Identifying Responsible Parties: Accountability mechanisms should clearly define who is responsible for the development, deployment, and maintenance of AI systems. This becomes challenging as AI systems become more autonomous and complex.

- Error Correction and Recourse: Establishing procedures for error correction and providing recourse for individuals affected by AI decisions are essential aspects of accountability. Users should have avenues for redress in case of system errors or misuse.
- Transparency as a Tool for Accountability: Transparency plays a vital role in accountability. Openly sharing information about how AI systems operate helps identify responsible parties and facilitates accountability measures.

Transparency:

Transparency in AI refers to the openness and explainability of AI systems. Transparent AI systems enable users to understand how decisions are made and why, fostering trust and accountability. Techniques such as explainable AI (XAI) aim to make AI algorithms more interpretable and transparent to stakeholders.

Achieving transparency in AI systems is challenging, particularly in deep learning models where the decision-making process is intricate. Balancing transparency with the need to protect proprietary algorithms is a delicate task. Researchers and practitioners are exploring ways to make AI systems more interpretable without compromising their effectiveness.

Exploration:

- Explainability of Decisions: Transparent AI systems provide explanations for their decisions. This is crucial, especially in high-stakes applications, where users need to understand why a particular decision was made.

- Interpretability of Models: The "black box" nature of some AI models can hinder transparency. Efforts should be made to enhance the interpretability of models, allowing users to comprehend and challenge the decision-making processes.
- User Understanding and Trust: Transparency builds user trust in AI systems. When users understand how AI systems operate, they are more likely to trust the technology. Trust is essential for the widespread adoption and acceptance of AI applications.

In summary, addressing bias, ensuring fairness, establishing accountability, and promoting transparency are critical considerations in the development and deployment of AI systems. Striking a balance among these principles is essential for creating ethical, trustworthy, and socially responsible AI technologies. Developers, policymakers, and stakeholders must work collaboratively to navigate these challenges and foster the responsible use of AI in various domains.

Chapter 6: Risks and Challenges in AI

As artificial intelligence (AI) continues to advance, it brings with it a host of risks and challenges that warrant careful consideration. This chapter explores the multifaceted landscape of risks associated with AI, ranging from societal concerns such as job displacement to technical challenges like the explainability and interpretability of AI systems. Additionally, we delve into the current and emerging safety measures designed to mitigate these risks and ensure responsible AI development.

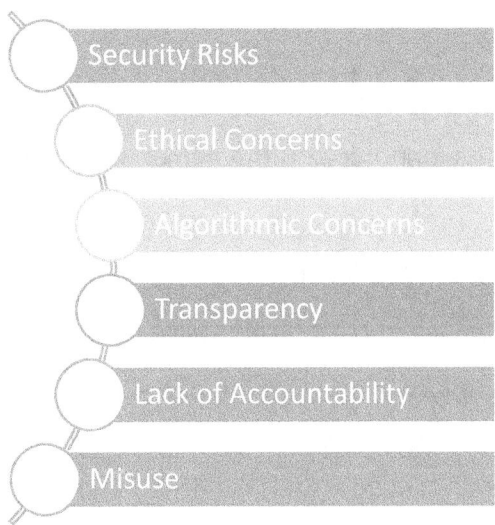

Potential Risks Associated with AI

Artificial Intelligence (AI) has the potential to bring about transformative changes in various domains, but it also poses certain risks that need careful consideration. Here are key potential risks associated with AI:

Job Displacement:

One of the primary concerns surrounding AI is the potential for job displacement due to automation. As AI systems become more proficient in tasks traditionally performed by humans, certain jobs may become obsolete. The impact on employment requires proactive measures to reskill and upskill the workforce to adapt to the evolving job market.

Overview:

One of the primary concerns surrounding AI is the potential for job displacement as a result of automation and increased efficiency. As AI systems become more proficient in tasks traditionally performed by humans, certain jobs may become obsolete, impacting various industries.

Potential Risks:

1. Skill Mismatch: Job displacement may lead to a mismatch between the skills of the existing workforce and the demands of the evolving job market.

2. Economic Disparities: Unequal distribution of job losses across different sectors may exacerbate economic disparities, affecting certain regions or demographics more than others.

Mitigation Strategies:

1. Reskilling Programs: Implement proactive reskilling and upskilling programs to equip the workforce with the skills needed for emerging job roles.

2. Collaboration with Industries: Foster collaboration between educational institutions, industries, and governments to identify and address emerging skill requirements.

Security Threats:

The increasing reliance on AI introduces new vectors for security threats. Malicious actors may exploit vulnerabilities in AI systems, leading to issues such as adversarial attacks, data manipulation, or the compromising of sensitive information. Strengthening AI security measures is crucial to safeguard against potential threats.

Overview:

The increasing reliance on AI introduces new vectors for security threats, posing risks to the integrity and confidentiality of AI systems and the data they process.

Potential Risks:

1. Adversarial Attacks: Malicious actors may manipulate input data to deceive AI systems, leading to incorrect or undesirable outcomes.

2. Data Manipulation: Security threats may involve unauthorized access to, or manipulation of, the data used to train AI models, compromising their accuracy and reliability.

Mitigation Strategies:

1. Robust Encryption: Implement robust encryption mechanisms to protect AI systems from unauthorized access and tampering.

2. Continuous Monitoring: Regularly monitor AI systems for anomalies or unexpected behavior, enabling the prompt identification and response to security threats.

Unintended Consequences:

The complexity of AI systems introduces the risk of unintended consequences. Biases in training data, algorithmic errors, or unforeseen interactions between AI components can result in unexpected outcomes. Understanding and mitigating these unintended consequences require thorough testing and ongoing monitoring of AI systems.

Overview:

The complexity of AI systems introduces the risk of unintended consequences, ranging from biases in decision-making to unforeseen interactions between AI components.

Potential Risks:

1. Biases in Training Data: AI systems may perpetuate and amplify biases present in training data, resulting in discriminatory outcomes.

2. Algorithmic Errors: Errors in the design or implementation of algorithms can lead to unintended and potentially harmful consequences.

Mitigation Strategies:

1. Diverse and Representative Training Data: Ensure that training data used for AI systems are diverse and representative to minimize biases.

2. Thorough Testing and Validation: Conduct extensive testing and validation to identify and address potential algorithmic errors before deployment.

Conclusion:

While AI holds tremendous potential, understanding and mitigating associated risks are paramount. Proactive measures, including reskilling programs, robust security protocols, and thorough testing, can help harness the benefits of AI while minimizing potential negative impacts on jobs, security, and unintended consequences. A holistic and responsible approach to AI development and deployment is essential for navigating challenges and ensuring a positive impact on society.

Ethical Concerns:

Overview:

AI applications raise ethical considerations related to fairness, accountability, transparency, and the potential misuse of technology.

Potential Risks:

1. Unfair Algorithmic Decisions: Biases in AI models may result in unfair or discriminatory outcomes, impacting individuals or communities.
2. Lack of Accountability: Clear lines of accountability for AI decision-making may be lacking, leading to challenges in addressing errors or ethical violations.

Mitigation Strategies:

1. Ethical AI Guidelines: Develop and adhere to ethical guidelines in AI development, emphasizing fairness, transparency, and accountability.
2. Regulatory Frameworks: Implement regulatory frameworks that govern the ethical use of AI and hold developers and organizations accountable.

In navigating the adoption of AI, stakeholders must strike a balance between harnessing its benefits and mitigating potential risks. Proactive measures, ethical considerations, and ongoing evaluation are essential for ensuring the responsible development and deployment of AI technologies.

Challenges of Explainability and Interpretability

Explainability:

The "black box" nature of some advanced AI algorithms raises challenges in explaining how decisions are made. This lack of transparency can lead to skepticism and hinder the acceptance of AI applications. Achieving explainability is crucial, especially in contexts where the impact of AI decisions is significant, such as healthcare, finance, and criminal justice.

Interpretability:

Interpretability is closely related to explainability but focuses on how well users can understand and trust the output of AI systems. As AI becomes more sophisticated, interpreting complex models like deep neural networks becomes challenging. Striking a balance between accuracy and interpretability is an ongoing challenge in AI research.

Explainability and interpretability are crucial aspects of Artificial Intelligence (AI) systems, ensuring that users, developers, and stakeholders can understand and trust the decisions made by AI models. However, these aspects pose certain challenges:

1. Complexity of Models:
   a. Challenge: Modern AI models, especially deep neural networks, are often complex and comprised of numerous layers and

parameters. Understanding the intricate relationships within these models can be challenging.

    b. Mitigation: Simplify models where possible, use visualization techniques to represent model internals, and provide high-level summaries of decision-making processes.

2. Black Box Nature:

    a. Challenge: Many AI models operate as black boxes, meaning their decision-making processes are not easily interpretable or explainable.

    b. Mitigation: Develop techniques for model transparency, such as opening the black box through interpretability tools, feature importance analysis, and attention mechanisms.

3. Trade-off Between Performance and Explainability:

    a. Challenge: There can be a trade-off between the accuracy of a model and its explainability. More complex models often achieve higher accuracy but are less interpretable.

    b. Mitigation: Strive for a balance by using models that offer a good compromise between accuracy and interpretability, or provide adjustable parameters to control the level of complexity.

4. Contextual Understanding:

    a. Challenge: AI models may lack a contextual understanding of the broader environment or domain, making their decisions difficult to interpret in specific situations.

    b. Mitigation: Enhance models with contextual information, domain-specific knowledge, or external data sources to improve their understanding of the environment.

5. Dynamic and Evolving Models:
   a. Challenge: Some AI models, particularly those utilizing reinforcement learning or continuous learning, can evolve and adapt over time, making it challenging to provide a static explanation.
   b. Mitigation: Implement continuous monitoring and update mechanisms to provide explanations that evolve with the model and its learning process.
6. Inherent Bias and Fairness Issues:
   a. Challenge: Biases present in training data can be perpetuated by AI models, leading to biased decisions. Explaining biased decisions requires addressing complex issues of fairness.
   b. Mitigation: Implement fairness-aware algorithms, thoroughly audit training data for biases, and actively work on mitigating bias through preprocessing or post-processing steps.
7. Legal and Ethical Considerations:
   a. Challenge: Regulations around the explainability of AI systems are evolving, and there may be legal and ethical considerations related to disclosing the inner workings of proprietary models.
   b. Mitigation: Adhere to ethical AI principles, comply with relevant regulations, and balance transparency with proprietary concerns.
8. User Understanding:
   a. Challenge: The intended audience, whether technical or non-technical, may have varying levels of understanding of AI concepts, making it challenging to provide explanations that cater to all users.

    b. Mitigation: Develop user-friendly interfaces, provide multiple levels of explanations, and use plain language to convey complex concepts.

9. Scalability:

    a. Challenge: As models become larger and more sophisticated, providing scalable explanations that remain comprehensible becomes challenging.

    b. Mitigation: Utilize visualization techniques, focus on high-impact explanations, and develop scalable tools for interpreting model outputs.

10. Robustness and Security:

    a. Challenge: Explaining models can potentially expose vulnerabilities or be exploited by malicious actors to reverse-engineer models.

    b. Mitigation: Balance transparency with security considerations, implement secure systems, and use techniques like model distillation to create simplified, secure versions for explanation.

Addressing these challenges requires a multidisciplinary approach involving researchers, practitioners, ethicists, and policymakers to develop standards, tools, and best practices for explainable and interpretable AI systems. Continuous efforts are essential to ensure AI technology aligns with human values, ethics, and regulatory requirements.

Overview of Current and Emerging AI Safety Measures

Ensuring the safety of Artificial Intelligence (AI) systems is paramount to their responsible development and deployment. Several measures and initiatives have emerged to address ethical concerns, regulatory oversight, safety research, explainability, robustness, and collaboration.

Ethical Guidelines and Standards:

International organizations and industry bodies have introduced ethical guidelines and standards to guide the development and deployment of AI. Initiatives such as the IEEE Global Initiative on Ethics of Autonomous and Intelligent Systems provide frameworks to ensure responsible AI practices.

Overview:

- Ethical guidelines serve as foundational principles guiding the development and use of AI technologies.
- Organizations and research institutions have developed ethical frameworks to promote responsible AI practices.

Key Aspects:

- Fairness and Bias Mitigation: Guidelines emphasize the need to address biases and promote fairness in AI systems.
- Transparency and Accountability: Encourages transparent AI development and accountability for system behavior.
- Privacy and Security: Highlights the importance of protecting user privacy and securing AI systems against potential threats.

Regulatory Oversight:

Governments and regulatory bodies are actively engaging in the development of AI regulations to address safety concerns. Regulatory frameworks aim to set standards for transparency, accountability, and security in AI systems, providing a basis for ethical AI development.

Overview:

- Governments and international bodies are increasingly recognizing the need for regulatory frameworks to govern AI development and deployment.
- Regulatory oversight aims to set standards, ensure compliance, and safeguard against potential risks.

Key Aspects:

- Data Protection and Privacy Regulations: Regulations emphasize the responsible handling of user data, ensuring privacy rights are protected.
- Anti-discrimination Measures: Address concerns related to algorithmic biases and discrimination.
- Algorithmic Accountability: Enforce accountability for the decisions made by AI systems, especially in critical applications.

AI Safety Research:

Ongoing research in AI safety is crucial for identifying and addressing potential risks. Researchers are exploring methods to enhance the robustness of AI algorithms, prevent adversarial attacks, and improve the explainability of complex models.

- Ongoing research focuses on identifying potential risks and vulnerabilities in AI systems.

- Researchers work towards developing methodologies to enhance the safety and reliability of AI technologies.

Key Aspects:

- Identification of Bias and Fairness Issues: Research aims to uncover biases in AI models and propose solutions to mitigate them.
- Examination of Adversarial Attacks: Investigates vulnerabilities to adversarial attacks and develops defenses against them.
- Continuous Monitoring and Updates: Focuses on creating AI systems that can adapt to changing conditions and improve over time.

Explainable AI (XAI) Techniques:

Explainable AI techniques focus on developing models that provide clear and understandable explanations for their decisions. This includes techniques such as rule-based models, interpretable machine learning models, and methods for visualizing complex neural network architectures.

Overview:

- Explainable AI (XAI) techniques aim to make AI systems more interpretable, allowing users to understand their decisions.
- Enhances transparency and user trust in AI algorithms.

Key Aspects:

- Interpretability Tools: Development of tools that provide insights into the decision-making process of AI models.

- Feature Importance Analysis: Techniques to identify the features influencing AI decisions.
- User-Friendly Interfaces: Creation of interfaces that present complex AI concepts in a comprehensible manner.

Robustness and Adversarial Training:

To address security threats and unintended consequences, researchers are actively working on improving the robustness of AI systems. Adversarial training involves exposing AI models to potential attack scenarios during training, making them more resilient to adversarial attempts.

Overview:

- Robustness measures focus on making AI systems resistant to adversarial attacks and ensuring reliable performance in various conditions.
- Adversarial training involves training models with adversarial examples to improve resilience.

Key Aspects:

- Adversarial Training Techniques: Integrating adversarial examples during the training phase to enhance model robustness.
- Regularization Methods: Incorporating regularization techniques to reduce model sensitivity to perturbations.
- Security-Aware Development: Implementing security measures throughout the AI development lifecycle.

Collaboration and Open Source Initiatives:

Collaboration among researchers, industry practitioners, and policymakers is essential for addressing AI risks collectively. Open source initiatives and collaborative platforms foster the sharing of knowledge, tools, and best practices to enhance AI safety measures.

Overview:

- Collaboration between industry, academia, and government promotes the exchange of knowledge and best practices.
- Open source initiatives contribute to the development of shared resources and tools for enhancing AI safety.

Key Aspects:

- Knowledge Sharing: Collaboration platforms facilitate the exchange of safety insights and methodologies.
- Open Source Safety Tools: Development and sharing of tools to assess, monitor, and improve the safety of AI systems.
- Community Engagement: Involvement of diverse stakeholders in open discussions and initiatives related to AI safety.

These current and emerging AI safety measures reflect a collective effort to address ethical, regulatory, and technical challenges. As AI technologies continue to evolve, ongoing research, collaboration, and the implementation of robust safety measures will be crucial to ensuring the responsible and beneficial integration of AI into various domains.

Conclusion

The risks and challenges associated with AI require a holistic and collaborative approach. As we navigate the complexities of job displacement, security threats, and unintended consequences, it is imperative to prioritize ethical considerations and implement safety measures. The ongoing evolution of AI safety research, coupled with regulatory oversight and industry best practices, will contribute to the responsible development and deployment of AI technologies. By addressing these challenges head-on, we can unlock the full potential of AI while minimizing associated risks and ensuring a positive impact on society.

Section 2: AI Governance

AI is transforming the world in unprecedented ways, from enhancing productivity and innovation to creating new challenges and risks. As AI becomes more powerful and ubiquitous, it is essential to ensure that it is aligned with human values and interests and that it is used responsibly and ethically. This is the goal of AI governance, which refers to the set of policies, principles, norms, standards, and practices that guide the development and deployment of AI systems.

Chapter 7: The Need for AI Governance

- Introduction to the concept of AI governance and its significance.

- Overview of existing AI governance frameworks and regulatory initiatives.
- Importance of collaboration between governments, industries, and academia in shaping effective AI governance.

Chapter 8: Understanding AI Governance

- Introduction to the concept of AI governance and its significance.
- Overview of existing AI governance frameworks and regulatory initiatives.

Chapter 9: Building Responsible AI Systems

- Discussion on the principles of responsible AI development.
- Consideration of human-centric design and the importance of user privacy.

Chapter 10: Stakeholders in AI Governance

- Main Stakeholder: Government, private sector, Academia, non-profits and other organizations
- Collaboration between the actors

Chapter 11: Mechanisms and Tools for AI Governance

- Tools and approaches to achieve AI Governance

By the end of this Section, you will have a comprehensive understanding of the concept and scope of AI governance, as well as its main opportunities and challenges. You will also learn about some of the best practices and examples of AI governance tools for effective AI Governance.

Chapter 7: The Need for AI Governance

Artificial Intelligence (AI) stands at the forefront of technological innovation, bringing about transformative changes in various aspects of our lives. With this technological revolution, the concept of AI governance has emerged as a critical framework to ensure responsible development, deployment, and ethical use of AI systems. This chapter explores the significance of AI governance, provides an overview of existing frameworks and regulatory initiatives, and emphasizes the crucial role of collaboration between governments, industries, and academia in shaping effective AI governance.

AI Governance: A Conceptual Overview

Defining AI Governance

The term "AI governance" encompasses a set of policies, guidelines, and ethical considerations that guide the development and utilization of AI technologies. It aims to strike a balance between fostering innovation and addressing the ethical, societal, and legal implications of AI. AI governance is essential for ensuring that AI systems align with human values, respect privacy, and operate transparently.

Significance of AI Governance

The significance of AI governance lies in its ability to mitigate risks, promote accountability, and safeguard against unintended consequences associated with AI technologies. It serves as a compass to navigate the complex ethical and regulatory landscape surrounding AI, fostering public trust and responsible innovation.

Overview of Existing AI Governance Frameworks

AI governance frameworks provide guidelines and principles to ensure the responsible development and deployment of Artificial Intelligence (AI) technologies. Several organizations and initiatives have developed frameworks to address ethical, legal, and societal considerations associated with AI.

European Union's AI Act

The European Union has emerged as a pioneer in AI governance with the introduction of the AI Act. Categorizing AI systems based on risk levels, the regulation imposes stringent requirements on high-risk applications, emphasizing transparency, accountability, and the prohibition of specific practices.

The European Union's AI Act, introduced in 2021, is a pioneering regulatory framework. It categorizes AI systems based on risk levels, imposing stringent requirements on high-risk applications. The Act emphasizes transparency, accountability, and the prohibition of certain high-risk practices, setting a precedent for comprehensive AI regulation.

United States: Decentralized Framework and Sector-Specific Regulations

In the United States, AI governance is characterized by a decentralized approach, with existing laws and guidelines governing AI applications across various sectors. The Federal Trade Commission (FTC) plays a role in enforcing fairness and transparency in AI systems. The Federal Trade Commission (FTC) plays a role in enforcing However, the absence of a comprehensive federal framework highlights the challenges in maintaining consistency across industries.

China's Strategic Initiatives

China has outlined ambitious plans for AI dominance by 2030, introducing guidelines and policies to shape the development and deployment of AI technologies. These initiatives underscore the dynamic nature of China's regulatory environment in response to technological advancements.

China has outlined ambitious plans to become a global AI leader by 2030. The government has introduced guidelines and policies addressing data security, AI standards, and ethical considerations. China's regulatory environment reflects its commitment to responsible AI development while fostering innovation.

Global Collaboration: OECD and UNESCO

International organizations, such as the Organization for Economic Co-operation and Development (OECD) and the United Nations Educational, Scientific and Cultural Organization (UNESCO), contribute to the global AI governance landscape. The OECD's AI Principles emphasize human-centric values, while UNESCO engages in discussions on the ethical dimensions of AI.

International organizations, such as the Organization for Economic Co-operation and Development (OECD) and the United Nations Educational, Scientific and Cultural Organization (UNESCO), contribute to global AI governance. The OECD's AI Principles emphasize human-centric values, transparency, and accountability, providing a foundation for ethical AI development.

Importance of Collaboration

Collaboration is crucial in various contexts, and it plays a pivotal role in ensuring the responsible development, deployment, and governance of Artificial Intelligence (AI).

Government-Industry Collaboration

Effective AI governance requires collaboration between governments and industries. Governments play a pivotal role in setting regulatory frameworks, while industries are responsible for implementing ethical practices in AI development and deployment. This collaboration ensures that AI technologies align with societal values and legal standards.

Academia's Contribution

Academia plays a pivotal role in researching and developing ethical AI practices. Collaboration between academia, industry, and government facilitates knowledge exchange, promotes best practices, and addresses emerging challenges. Academic institutions contribute valuable insights to inform AI governance frameworks.

Cross-Border Collaboration

Cross-border collaboration is crucial in creating a cohesive global AI governance framework. The challenges of aligning diverse regulatory approaches highlight the need for international cooperation to address the global impact of AI. Collaborative efforts between nations help create a cohesive global AI governance framework, acknowledging regional differences while promoting universally accepted ethical standards. International cooperation fosters a shared commitment to responsible AI development.

Challenges in Implementing Effective AI Governance

Implementing effective AI governance faces several challenges due to the rapid evolution of technology, ethical considerations, and the global nature of AI.

Ethical Considerations

The ethical considerations in AI governance involve striking a balance between innovation and societal values. Addressing bias, ensuring fairness, and promoting transparency and accountability are paramount to effective AI governance.

Regulatory Adaptability

The challenge of creating adaptive regulatory frameworks that can keep pace with the rapidly evolving AI landscape requires regulatory agility. Adaptable frameworks are necessary to address emerging risks and opportunities in AI development.

Striking a Global Balance

Achieving a global balance in AI governance involves navigating the complexities of harmonizing regulations across diverse cultural, legal, and economic contexts. Strategies for balancing global approaches while respecting regional differences are crucial.

Future Directions and Recommendations

The rapid advancement of AI technologies necessitates the evolution of governance models to effectively address emerging challenges.

Evolving Governance Models

The future of AI governance may witness the evolution of governance models to address the dynamic nature of AI technologies. Anticipating, continuous research and adaptation of governance frameworks will be essential to stay ahead of emerging challenges.

- Agile Governance Frameworks: Develop flexible governance frameworks capable of adapting to the evolving landscape of AI technologies. These frameworks should incorporate mechanisms for continuous monitoring, assessment, and updates to ensure relevance and effectiveness.
- Anticipatory Governance: Proactively anticipate future AI developments and potential risks through robust research and scenario planning. Establish mechanisms for early detection of emerging issues and agile responses to mitigate risks.

- Dynamic Regulation: Move towards dynamic regulatory approaches that can swiftly respond to technological advancements while upholding ethical principles and safeguarding societal interests. Foster collaboration between policymakers, industry stakeholders, and researchers to develop responsive regulatory frameworks.

Multidisciplinary Collaboration

A call to action for increased collaboration between government agencies, industries, academia, and international organizations. A multidisciplinary approach ensures a holistic perspective, fostering a comprehensive understanding of the ethical, societal, and technological dimensions of AI governance.

- Cross-Sector Partnerships: Facilitate partnerships between government agencies, industry players, academic institutions, and civil society organizations to pool resources, share expertise, and develop comprehensive AI governance strategies.
- Interdisciplinary Research: Promote interdisciplinary research initiatives that bring together experts from various fields, including computer science, ethics, law, sociology, and psychology. Encourage collaboration to address the multifaceted challenges of AI governance.
- International Cooperation: Foster international collaboration and information-sharing networks to promote harmonization of AI governance standards, exchange best practices, and address global challenges collectively. Engage in diplomatic efforts to establish common principles and frameworks for ethical AI development and deployment.

- Public Engagement: Involve the public in AI governance processes through participatory mechanisms, such as public consultations, citizen assemblies, and stakeholder forums. Foster transparency, accountability, and inclusivity in decision-making to build public trust and legitimacy.

By embracing evolving governance models and fostering multidisciplinary collaboration, stakeholders can navigate the complex challenges of AI governance and pave the way for responsible, inclusive, and beneficial AI development and deployment. These recommendations aim to ensure that AI technologies serve the common good while upholding fundamental ethical principles and respecting human rights.

Conclusion

In conclusion, the need for AI governance arises from the transformative impact of AI on society. The conceptual framework of AI governance, as evidenced by existing initiatives, underscores the importance of ethical considerations, transparency, and collaboration. As we navigate the complexities of AI, a collaborative and adaptive approach to governance is crucial to ensure responsible innovation and the positive integration of AI into our global society. The continued commitment to ethical AI practices and international collaboration will pave the way for a future where AI benefits humanity at large.

Recapitulation of Key Points

Summarizing the significance of AI governance in guiding responsible AI development, mitigating risks, and fostering ethical innovation.

Vision for Responsible AI Future

Emphasizing the call to action for stakeholders to prioritize responsible AI practices, engage in ongoing research, dialogue, and collaboration to ensure a positive and ethical future for artificial intelligence.

Chapter 8: What is AI Governance?

AI governance is the process of establishing and enforcing rules, norms, standards, and principles for the development, deployment, and use of AI systems. AI governance aims to ensure that AI is trustworthy, responsible, fair, transparent, accountable, and beneficial for humanity. AI governance also seeks to address the potential harms and negative consequences of AI, such as bias, discrimination, privacy violations, misinformation, manipulation, and weaponization. AI governance involves multiple stakeholders, such as AI developers, users, policymakers, regulators, ethicists, and civil society groups, who have different roles and responsibilities in shaping the behavior and impact of AI systems.

AI governance is important for several reasons. First, it can help to prevent or mitigate the potential harms of AI, such as unfair or inaccurate decisions, violations of human rights or dignity, or threats to public safety or security. Second, it can help to foster trust and confidence in AI among the public and the users by ensuring that AI systems are transparent, explainable, accountable, and aligned with human values. Third, it can help to promote innovation and progress in AI by creating a conducive environment for research and development and by addressing the legal and ethical issues that may arise from the use of AI.

There are different approaches and frameworks for AI governance, depending on the context, scope, and objectives of the governance. Some examples are:

- **Ethical principles and guidelines**: These are high-level statements that express the values and norms that should guide the design and use of AI. They are often derived from existing ethical frameworks or human rights declarations. For example, the European Commission has proposed seven key requirements for trustworthy AI: human agency and oversight; technical robustness and safety; privacy and data governance; transparency; diversity, non-discrimination, and fairness; societal and environmental well-being; and accountability.

- **Technical standards and best practices**: These are more specific and operational rules that define the technical requirements and methods for ensuring the quality and performance of AI systems. They are often developed by professional associations or standardization bodies. For example, the IEEE has developed a series of standards for ethically aligned design of autonomous and intelligent systems.

- **Legal regulations and oversight mechanisms**: These are binding rules that establish the legal obligations and liabilities of the actors involved in the development and use of AI. They are often enacted by governments or international organizations. For example, the European Union has proposed a regulation on artificial intelligence that sets out a risk-based approach to regulating different types of AI applications.

- **Multi-stakeholder initiatives and partnerships**: These are collaborative efforts that involve various actors from different sectors and backgrounds who share a common vision or goal for AI governance. They are often voluntary or self-regulatory in nature. For example, the Partnership on AI is a global coalition of organizations that works to ensure that AI is used for social good.

AI governance is an evolving and dynamic field that requires constant monitoring, evaluation, and adaptation to the changing technological landscape and societal needs. It also requires a global perspective and coordination to address the cross-border implications and challenges of AI. By engaging in AI governance, we can shape the future of AI in a way that reflects our collective values and aspirations.

Examples of AI Governance

To illustrate the concept of AI governance, here are some examples of how it can be applied in different domains and contexts:

-   **Healthcare**: AI governance can help to ensure that AI applications in healthcare, such as diagnosis, treatment, or drug discovery, are safe, effective, and respectful of the privacy and autonomy of patients and healthcare providers. For example, the World Health Organization has developed a global strategy on digital health that includes ethical and governance principles for digital health technologies.
-   **Education**: AI governance can help to ensure that AI applications in education, such as personalized learning, assessment, or tutoring, are fair, inclusive, and supportive of the learning outcomes and well-being of students and educators. For example, the UNESCO has adopted a recommendation on the ethics of artificial intelligence that covers the use of AI in education and other fields.
-   **Environment**: AI governance can help to ensure that AI applications in environment, such as climate modeling, disaster management, or

conservation, are sustainable, responsible, and aligned with the environmental goals and values of society. For example, the UN Environment Program has launched a digital transformation initiative that aims to leverage AI and other technologies for environmental action.

- **Security**: AI governance can help to ensure that AI applications in security, such as surveillance, cyber defense, or warfare, are lawful, ethical, and accountable for their actions and consequences. For example, the UN Secretary-General has called for a global ban on lethal autonomous weapons systems that can select and engage targets without human intervention.

These examples show that AI governance is a diverse and complex field that requires a context-specific and multi-dimensional approach. It also requires a global perspective and coordination to address the cross-border implications and challenges of AI. By engaging in AI governance, we can shape the future of AI in a way that reflects our collective values and aspirations.

Chapter 9: Building Responsible AI Systems

As artificial intelligence (AI) technologies continue to advance, there is a growing imperative to prioritize responsible development practices. Building AI systems that are ethical, transparent, and accountable is essential to ensure they benefit society while minimizing potential harms. This chapter explores the principles of responsible AI development, emphasizes human-centric design, and underscores the importance of protecting user privacy. Through case studies, we highlight successful implementations of responsible AI practices in various domains.

The Imperative of Responsible AI

- The growing importance of incorporating responsible practices in AI development.
- The impact of responsible AI on user trust, ethical considerations, and societal benefits.

.

Principles of Responsible AI Development

- An overview of key principles guiding the responsible development of AI systems.
- Balancing innovation with ethical considerations, transparency, and accountability.

Ethical Considerations

Responsible AI development starts with a commitment to ethical principles. This includes fairness, transparency, accountability, and respect for human rights. Ethical guidelines provide a framework for ensuring that AI systems align with societal values and do not perpetuate biases or discrimination.

Transparency and Explainability

Transparency and explainability are essential for fostering trust in AI systems. Users should understand how AI decisions are made and be able to challenge or verify them. Transparent AI systems provide insights into their inner workings, enabling users to assess their reliability and fairness.

Accountability and Oversight

Accountability mechanisms are necessary to hold developers and users of AI systems responsible for their actions. This includes establishing clear lines of responsibility, implementing robust governance structures, and providing avenues for recourse in case of harm or misuse. Regulatory oversight ensures compliance with ethical and legal standards.

Human-Centric Design in Responsible AI

Human-centric design prioritizes the needs, values, and experiences of end-users. AI systems should be designed with empathy and consideration for diverse perspectives. User involvement throughout the development process helps identify potential biases, usability issues, and ethical concerns.

Understanding Human-Centric Design

- The significance of prioritizing user needs, values, and experiences in AI design.
- The role of empathy and inclusivity in creating AI systems that enhance human well-being.

User Privacy as a Fundamental Right

- The importance of safeguarding user privacy in AI development.
- Strategies for implementing privacy-preserving measures without compromising functionality.

Protecting user privacy is paramount in AI development. This involves minimizing data collection, implementing robust security measures, and obtaining informed consent for data usage. Privacy-enhancing technologies, such as differential privacy and federated learning, enable AI systems to learn from data without compromising individual privacy.

Ethical Considerations in Human-Centric AI

- Addressing ethical dilemmas related to AI impact on individuals and communities.
- Ensuring fairness, avoiding bias, and promoting inclusivity in AI algorithms.

Challenges in Building Responsible AI Systems

Ethical Dilemmas and Trade-offs

- Discussion on the challenges of navigating ethical dilemmas and trade-offs in AI development.
- Balancing the benefits of innovation with potential risks and societal impact.

Technical Complexity and Explainability

- Addressing the technical complexities in building responsible AI systems.
- The challenge of ensuring the explainability of complex AI models to enhance user understanding.

Global Variations in Regulatory Standards

- Navigating the variations in AI regulatory standards across different regions.
- Strategies for building AI systems that adhere to diverse legal and ethical frameworks.

Future Directions and Continuous Improvement

The Evolving Landscape of Responsible AI

- Anticipating future challenges and opportunities in responsible AI development.
- The importance of continuous learning, adaptation, and ethical evolution in AI systems.

Community Engagement and User Empowerment

- The role of community engagement in shaping responsible AI systems.
- Strategies for empowering users to make informed decisions about AI interactions.

Conclusion

Building responsible AI systems requires a multifaceted approach that prioritizes ethical considerations, human-centric design, and user privacy. By adhering to principles such as fairness, transparency, accountability, and privacy preservation, developers can create AI technologies that benefit society while minimizing potential harms. As AI continues to evolve, a commitment to responsible development is essential to ensure its positive impact on individuals, communities, and society as a whole.

Recapitulation of Key Principles

- Summarizing the principles of responsible AI development.
- Emphasizing the importance of human-centric design, user privacy, and ethical considerations.

The Path Forward

- Encouraging a collective commitment to building responsible AI systems.
- The role of collaboration, transparency, and ethical consciousness in shaping the future of AI development for the benefit of humanity.

Chapter 10: Stakeholders in AI governance

AI governance is a complex and multidimensional challenge that requires the participation and cooperation of various actors and stakeholders. It is important to understand who are the main players in the field of AI governance, what are their roles and interests, and how can we foster collaboration and coordination among them.

The main actors and stakeholders involved in AI governance can be broadly categorized into four groups: governments, the private sector, civil society, and academia. Each of these groups has different perspectives, motivations, and capabilities regarding the development, deployment, and regulation of AI systems.

Governments

Governments are responsible for setting the legal and policy frameworks that govern the use of AI in their jurisdictions. They also have the power to fund and support AI research and innovation, as well as to ensure the protection of public interests, such as human rights, security, and social welfare. Governments face the challenge of balancing the benefits and risks of AI, as well as harmonizing their national policies with international norms and standards.

Private Sector

Private sector actors include companies, entrepreneurs, investors, and developers who create, provide, and use AI products and services. They have a strong interest in advancing the state of the art of AI, as well as maximizing their economic gains and competitive advantages. Private sector actors also have a responsibility to ensure the quality, safety, and ethics of their AI solutions, as well as to respect the rights and interests of their customers, employees, and partners.

Non-Profits and Other Non-Governmental Organizations

Civil society actors include non-governmental organizations (NGOs), media, advocacy groups, professional associations, and individuals who represent the interests and values of various segments of society. They have a role in raising awareness, monitoring, and influencing the development and impact of AI on society. Civil society actors also have a stake in ensuring that AI is used for good purposes, that it respects human dignity and diversity, and that it promotes social justice and inclusion.

Education Sector

Academia actors include researchers, educators, students, and institutions who produce and disseminate knowledge about AI. They have a contribution to make in advancing the scientific and technical foundations of AI, as well as exploring its ethical, social, and cultural implications. Academia actors also have a duty to foster critical thinking, public education, and dialogue about AI among various stakeholders.

Collaboration Between Stakeholders

As we can see, AI governance is not a matter for a single actor or stakeholder group. Rather, it requires a collaborative and coordinated approach that involves multiple perspectives and interests. How can we foster such an approach? Here are some possible ways:

- Establishing multi-stakeholder platforms and forums that facilitate dialogue, consultation, and cooperation among different actors and stakeholders on AI governance issues.
- Developing common principles, guidelines, standards, and best practices that reflect shared values and goals for responsible AI.
- Creating mechanisms for transparency, accountability, oversight, and redress for AI systems that ensure their compliance with legal and ethical norms.
- Building capacity and literacy for all stakeholders to understand, engage with, and benefit from AI.
- Promoting inclusive and participatory processes that ensure the representation and empowerment of diverse voices and interests in AI governance.

AI governance is a collective endeavor that requires the involvement of all actors and stakeholders who have a stake in the future of AI. By working together, we can ensure that AI is developed and used in a way that serves the common good of humanity.

Chapter 11: Tools and Mechanisms for Implementing AI Governance

AI governance is a topic that has gained increasing attention in recent years, as artificial intelligence (AI) systems become more powerful, pervasive, and impactful. What are the main mechanisms and tools for implementing AI governance? There is no definitive answer to this question, as different contexts and challenges may require different approaches.

However, there are different mechanisms and tools that can help implement AI governance, depending on the level and scope of intervention.

Common Tools

Some of the common mechanisms and tools that have been proposed or adopted include:

AI ethics frameworks and principles

These are high-level statements of values and goals that provide guidance for AI development and use. Many organizations, such as governments, companies, academic institutions, and civil society groups, have developed their own AI ethics frameworks and principles, often drawing from existing human rights standards and ethical theories. Some examples are the OECD Principles on AI, the EU High-Level Expert Group on AI Ethics Guidelines, and the IEEE Ethically Aligned Design.

AI impact assessments:

These are systematic processes that aim to identify, assess, and mitigate the potential impacts of AI systems on human rights, society, environment, and other relevant domains. AI impact assessments can help ensure that AI systems are aligned with the intended outcomes and values, and that they do not cause unintended or adverse consequences.

AI standards and best practices:

These are more specific and operational guidelines that define the technical and procedural requirements for AI systems. They can cover various aspects of AI systems, such as data quality, algorithmic transparency, explainability, accountability, robustness, and security. Some examples are the ISO/IEC standards on AI, the Partnership on AI's Tenets, and the Responsible AI Practices by Google.

AI regulation and legislation:

These legal instruments establish the rules and obligations for AI development and use. They can address various issues related to AI systems, such as liability, privacy, data protection, consumer protection, intellectual property, and human rights. Some examples are the EU General Data Protection Regulation (GDPR), which has implications for AI systems that process personal data, the EU Proposal for a Regulation on Artificial Intelligence, which aims to create a harmonized legal framework for trustworthy AI in Europe, and the Algorithmic Accountability Act, which was introduced in the US Congress to require impact assessments for high-risk automated decision systems.

AI data governance:

This is the process of managing the quality, security, and accessibility of data used for training and testing AI systems. Data governance ensures that data is accurate, representative, unbiased, and compliant with relevant laws and regulations. It also involves ensuring that data subjects have control over their personal data and can exercise their rights to access, correct, or delete it. For example, watsonx.governance is a platform that automates data governance to provide responsible, transparent, and explainable AI.

AI oversight and governance bodies:

These are institutions or organizations that monitor, evaluate, and advise on AI development and use. They can have various functions and powers, such as setting standards, conducting audits, providing recommendations, enforcing rules, or resolving disputes. They can also involve different types of actors, such as experts, regulators, policymakers, or civil society representatives. Some examples are the UK Centre for Data Ethics and Innovation, which provides independent advice to the UK government on data-driven technologies, including AI, the Global Partnership on Artificial Intelligence (GPAI), which is an international initiative that brings together experts from various sectors to support responsible and human-centric development and use of AI, and the Algorithmic Justice League, which is a non-profit organization that advocates for equitable and accountable AI.

These mechanisms and tools are not mutually exclusive or exhaustive. They can complement each other and be combined in different ways to achieve effective AI governance. The challenge is to find the right balance between innovation and regulation, between flexibility and accountability, and between diversity and coherence in governing AI.

Design Effective and Legitimate Mechanisms

AI mechanisms can be approached from different perspectives and levels.

Ethical principles and values:

What are the core values and principles that should guide the design and use of AI systems? How can we ensure that AI respects human dignity, autonomy, privacy, fairness, accountability, transparency, and social justice?

Legal frameworks and norms:

What are the existing laws and regulations that apply to AI systems? How can we update or create new laws and regulations that address the specific challenges and opportunities of AI? How can we harmonize the legal frameworks across different jurisdictions and regions?

Technical standards and best practices:

What are the technical methods and tools that can help ensure the quality, safety, reliability, security, and explainability of AI systems? How can we establish and enforce common standards and best practices for developing and testing AI systems?

Social impacts and implications:

What are the social consequences and implications of AI systems for individuals, groups, communities, and society at large? How can we assess and mitigate the potential negative impacts of AI, such as discrimination, bias, unemployment, polarization, or manipulation? How can we foster the positive impacts of AI, such as empowerment, inclusion, innovation, or education?

Mechanisms for AI Governance

As AI becomes more pervasive and powerful, we need to ensure that it aligns with our values and goals, and that it serves the common good. By engaging in informed and constructive dialogue, we can shape the future of AI in a way that reflects our collective vision and aspirations.

However, regulating and governing AI globally is not an easy task. There are many challenges and obstacles that hinder the development and implementation of a coherent and effective global framework for AI regulation, such as:

- The diversity and complexity of AI technology and its applications
- The lack of consensus and coordination among different stakeholders and actors
- The divergence and conflict of interests and values among different regions and countries

- The uncertainty and unpredictability of the future evolution and impact of AI
- The gap and imbalance of capabilities and resources among different regions and countries

Mechanisms

Institutions are the formal and informal rules, norms, and organizations that shape the behavior of actors and the outcomes of social interactions. They provide the structure and stability for collective action and cooperation, as well as the means for resolving conflicts and enforcing compliance. Institutions can be classified into different types according to their functions and characteristics, such as legal institutions (e.g., laws, courts), political institutions (e.g., governments, parliaments), economic institutions (e.g., markets, firms), social institutions (e.g., religions, cultures), or technical institutions (e.g., protocols, standards).

Regulations are a subset of legal institutions that specify the rules and obligations that actors have to follow when engaging in certain activities or domains. Regulations can be enacted by different authorities at different levels of governance, such as national governments, regional organizations, or international bodies. Regulations can also be complemented or substituted by self-regulation or co-regulation mechanisms, where actors voluntarily agree to adhere to certain norms or codes of conduct.

Standards are a subset of technical institutions that define the specifications and requirements that products or services have to meet in order to ensure their quality, compatibility, interoperability, safety, or performance. Standards can be developed by different actors from different sectors or domains, such as industry associations, professional organizations, academic institutions, or civil society groups. Standards can also be voluntary or mandatory depending on whether they are adopted by consensus or imposed by regulation.

Oversight mechanisms are the processes and procedures that monitor and evaluate the implementation and impact of institutions, regulations, and standards. Oversight mechanisms can involve different actors with different roles and responsibilities, such as regulators, auditors, inspectors, watchdogs, or whistleblowers. Oversight mechanisms can also use different methods and tools to collect and analyze data, such as inspections, audits, reports, surveys, or feedback mechanisms.

Some of the possible ways and means to overcome these challenges and to achieve a global regulation of AI, such as:

- The development and adoption of universal principles and norms for AI
- The establishment and strengthening of global institutions and mechanisms for AI
- The promotion and facilitation of global cooperation and dialogue on AI

- The integration and harmonization of regional and national frameworks for AI
- The empowerment and participation of diverse stakeholders and actors in AI

Some initiatives that exist today and are driving forces behind regulating AI globally, such as:

- The UN Secretary-General's Roadmap for Digital Cooperation
- The UNESCO Recommendation on the Ethics of Artificial Intelligence
- The OECD Principles on Artificial Intelligence
- The Global Partnership on Artificial Intelligence
- The IEEE Global Initiative on Ethics of Autonomous and Intelligent Systems

Section 3: Regulatory Space Around the World

Different countries and regions have different approaches to regulating AI, depending on their values, priorities, capabilities, and interests. Some have adopted comprehensive and horizontal frameworks that apply to all AI systems across sectors and domains, while others have opted for sector-specific and vertical regulations that target particular applications or use cases of AI. Some have focused on promoting innovation and competitiveness in AI, while others have emphasized protecting human dignity and fundamental rights in AI. Some have developed national strategies and action plans to guide their AI policies, while others have joined international initiatives and collaborations to harmonize their AI standards and norms.

In this section, we will provide an overview of the current state of AI regulations around the world, highlighting some of the key trends, challenges, and opportunities in this emerging field.

Chapter 12: Legal Frameworks Worldwide

- Examination of global efforts and collaborations in establishing AI governance standards.
- Comparison of AI governance frameworks in different countries.
- The role of international organizations in promoting ethical AI practices.

Chapter 13: Generative AI Regulation

Chapter 14: The Future of AI Governance

- Exploration of emerging trends and technologies that will impact AI governance.
- Potential scenarios and challenges in governing advanced AI systems.
- Strategies for adapting and evolving AI governance frameworks over time.

Chapter 15: The Future of AI Regulation

- Challenges and Opportunities

By the end of this Section, you will have a comprehensive understanding of the concept and scope of AI regulations that exist today, as well as its main opportunities and challenges. We will draw on examples from various countries and regions that have adopted or proposed AI regulation, such as the European Union (EU), the United Kingdom (UK), Brazil, China, and Japan.

Chapter 12: Legal Frameworks Worldwide

As AI becomes more widespread and impactful, many governments and organizations around the world are developing legal frameworks to regulate and govern its use. These legal frameworks aim to ensure that AI is used in a way that respects human dignity, rights, and values, and that it does not cause harm or injustice to humans or other entities.

However, these legal frameworks vary significantly in their scope, approach, and level of detail. Some of them focus on specific domains or applications of AI, such as health care, finance, or transportation. Others cover AI more broadly, addressing cross-cutting issues such as ethics, accountability, or transparency. Some of them are binding and enforceable, such as laws or regulations. Others are voluntary and advisory, such as guidelines or standards.

The EU Approach: A Comprehensive and Risk-Based Framework

The EU has been a pioneer in developing a comprehensive and risk-based framework for AI regulation. In April 2021, the European Commission published a proposal for an Artificial Intelligence Act (AIA), which aims to create a legal framework for trustworthy and human-centric AI in the EU. The AIA defines AI as "a system that is software-based or that is embedded in hardware devices, and that displays behavior simulating intelligence by processing data or content through machine learning or other approaches such as logic- and knowledge-based approaches".

The AI Act adopts a risk-based approach to regulating AI, distinguishing between four categories of AI systems: prohibited, high-risk, limited-risk, and minimal-risk. Prohibited AI systems are those that violate fundamental rights or values, such as social scoring systems or systems that manipulate human behavior. High-risk AI systems are those that pose significant threats to safety or fundamental rights in certain sectors or contexts, such as health care, education, law enforcement, or biometric identification. Limited-risk AI systems are those that pose some risks to fundamental rights but do not qualify as high-risk, such as chatbots or deepfakes. Minimal-risk AI systems are those that pose no or negligible risks to fundamental rights or safety, such as video games or spam filters.

The AI Act imposes different obligations on different actors involved in the AI lifecycle, such as providers, users, importers, or distributors. For high-risk AI systems, the obligations include conducting a risk assessment, ensuring data quality and traceability, implementing technical and human oversight mechanisms, ensuring transparency and information provision to users, ensuring accuracy and robustness of the system's performance, and registering the system in an EU database. For limited-risk AI systems, the main obligation is to ensure transparency and information provision to users. For minimal-risk AI systems, no specific obligations apply.

The AI Act also establishes an EU-wide governance structure for AI regulation, involving various bodies and actors at different levels. These include the EC as the main policy-maker and enforcer of the rules; the European Artificial Intelligence Board (EAIB) as an independent advisory body composed of representatives from national authorities and the European Data Protection Board (EDPB); national competent authorities as responsible for supervising and enforcing compliance with the rules at the national level; notified bodies as private entities designated by national authorities to assess conformity of high-risk AI systems with the requirements; and market surveillance authorities as responsible for monitoring compliance of AI systems placed on the market.

The EU's approach to AI regulation is ambitious and comprehensive, aiming to set global standards for ethical and trustworthy AI. However, it also faces some challenges and criticisms, such as its complexity and potential burden for innovation; its lack of clarity on some key concepts and definitions; its possible conflicts with other existing or emerging legal frameworks; its potential fragmentation due to national variations in implementation; and its effectiveness in addressing global challenges posed by non-EU actors.

The UK Approach: A Sectoral and Principles-Based Regulation
The UK has adopted a sectoral and principles-based approach to regulating AI, relying on existing laws and regulators to address the specific issues and challenges posed by AI in different domains. For example, the Information Commissioner's Office (ICO) is responsible for overseeing data protection and privacy issues related to AI; the Equality and Human Rights Commission (EHRC) is responsible for ensuring non-discrimination and equality in the use of AI; the

Competition and Markets Authority (CMA) is responsible for promoting fair competition and consumer protection in relation to AI; and the Financial Conduct Authority (FCA) is responsible for regulating financial services that use AI.

The UK has also developed several principles and guidelines for the ethical and responsible use of AI across different sectors. For instance, in 2018, the UK government published a Data Ethics Framework to guide the design and use of data-driven technologies in the public sector. In 2019, the ICO published Guidance on Artificial Intelligence and Data Protection to help organizations comply with their data protection obligations when using AI. In 2020, the Centre for Data Ethics and Innovation (CDEI) published an AI Barometer to identify the most pressing opportunities and risks of AI in five sectors: criminal justice, financial services, health and social care, digital/online platforms, and energy and utilities. In 2021, the Alan Turing Institute published a Guide to Using Artificial Intelligence in the Public Sector to help public sector organizations implement AI ethically and safely.

In 2023, UK's Department for Science, Innovation and Technology has published a framework that underpins five principles to guide and inform the responsible development and use of AI in all sectors of the economy:

- Safety, security and robustness
- Appropriate transparency and explainability
- Fairness
- Accountability and governance

- Contestability and redress

The US Approach: A Fragmented and Enforcement-Based Regulation

In late 2023, White House signed Executive Order 14110 on Safe, Secure, and Trustworthy Artificial Intelligence. The EO's mandate to protect Americans from the potential risks of AI systems:

- Managing risks to safety and security
- Innovating AI for good

Before this EO, the US has a fragmented and enforcement-based approach to regulating AI, relying on existing laws and agencies to address the potential harms and benefits of AI in various contexts. Unlike the EU or the UK, the US does not have comprehensive or sectoral regulation for AI, nor does it have a dedicated regulator or agency for overseeing AI. Instead, the US has a patchwork of federal, state, and local laws and regulations that may apply to AI in different ways, depending on the specific use case, sector, or jurisdiction.

Some of the federal laws and agencies that may be relevant for regulating AI in the US include: the Federal Trade Commission Act (FTC Act) and the Federal Trade Commission (FTC), which prohibit unfair or deceptive acts or practices in commerce and enforce consumer protection and antitrust laws; the Civil Rights Act of 1964 and the Equal Employment Opportunity Commission (EEOC), which prohibit discrimination on the basis of race, color, religion, sex, or national origin in employment; the Fair Credit Reporting Act (FCRA) and the

Consumer Financial Protection Bureau (CFPB), which regulate consumer credit reporting and protect consumers from unfair, deceptive, or abusive practices in financial services; the Health Insurance Portability and Accountability Act (HIPAA) and the Department of Health and Human Services (HHS), which protect the privacy and security of health information; and the National Defense Authorization Act (NDAA) and the Department of Defense (DoD), which authorize and fund military activities and research related to AI.

The US has also developed some principles and guidelines for promoting trustworthy and innovative AI across different sectors. For example, in 2019, the White House published an Executive Order on Maintaining American Leadership in Artificial Intelligence, which established a national strategy for advancing AI research and development, fostering public trust and engagement, protecting civil liberties and privacy, enhancing national security and economic competitiveness, and promoting international cooperation. In 2020, the Office of Management and Budget (OMB) published a Guidance for Regulation of Artificial Intelligence Applications, which provided agencies with a set of principles for regulating AI applications in a manner that fosters innovation, growth, public trust, and public participation. In 2021, the National Institute of Standards and Technology (NIST) published a Framework for Improving Critical Infrastructure Cybersecurity: Version 1.1, which included a new section on managing cybersecurity risks posed by AI systems.

The Canadian Approach: A Collaborative and Human-Centric Regulation

Canada has adopted a collaborative and human-centric approach to regulating AI, emphasizing the importance of engaging with various stakeholders and respecting human rights and values in the development and use of AI. Canada does not have a specific law or regulation for AI, but it has several existing laws and regulators that may apply to AI in different contexts. For example, the Personal Information Protection and Electronic Documents Act (PIPEDA) and the Office of the Privacy Commissioner of Canada (OPC) regulate the collection, use, and disclosure of personal information in commercial activities; the Canadian Human Rights Act and the Canadian Human Rights Commission (CHRC) protect individuals from discrimination on prohibited grounds in employment and services; the Competition Act and the Competition Bureau enforce competition law and promote fair business practices; and the Access to Information Act and the Information Commissioner of Canada (OIC) provide access to information held by federal institutions.

Canada has also developed several initiatives and frameworks for fostering ethical and responsible use of AI across different sectors. For instance, in 2017, Canada co-launched with France the Global Partnership on Artificial Intelligence (GPAI), an international initiative that brings together experts from government, industry, civil society, and academia to support the responsible development and use of AI globally. In 2019, the Treasury Board Secretariat published a Directive on Automated Decision-Making, which established rules and guidelines for using automated decision systems in federal government operations. In 2020, the Canadian Council of Innovators published an AI Playbook, which provided practical guidance for Canadian businesses to adopt

AI solutions. In 2021, the Standards Council of Canada published a National Standard of Canada for Ethical Design and Use of Automated Decision Systems, which provided a framework for ensuring that AI systems are aligned with human values and respect human rights.

The AI Playbook is a comprehensive guide that covers the entire AI lifecycle, from identifying the problem and defining the objectives, to developing, deploying, and monitoring the solution. It also provides best practices and recommendations for each stage, such as how to assess the feasibility and readiness of AI projects, how to select the right data sources and methods, how to ensure data quality and security, how to test and validate the results, how to communicate and explain the outcomes, and how to measure the impact and value of AI solutions.

The Ethical Design and Use of Automated Decision Systems standard is a voluntary standard that aims to promote trust and confidence in AI systems. It defines a set of principles and requirements for designing, developing, deploying, and using AI systems that respect human dignity, autonomy, fairness, transparency, accountability, and privacy. It also provides guidance on how to conduct ethical assessments and audits of AI systems, how to establish governance structures and processes for oversight and review, and how to engage with stakeholders and users.

Both documents are complementary and can be used together to support Canadian organizations in their AI journey. By following the AI Playbook, organizations can ensure that they have a clear vision and strategy for AI adoption, that they have the necessary skills and resources, that they follow a rigorous and robust methodology, and that they deliver high-quality and reliable solutions. By following the Ethical Design and Use of Automated Decision Systems standard, organizations can ensure that they adhere to ethical values and principles, that they protect human rights and interests, that they foster trust and transparency, and that they monitor and evaluate the impacts of their AI systems.

Collaboration: Canada recognizes that AI regulation cannot be done in isolation. It requires the engagement and cooperation of multiple stakeholders, such as governments, industry, academia, civil society, and the public. Canada has established various platforms and initiatives to facilitate dialogue and coordination among these actors, such as the Pan-Canadian AI Strategy, the Advisory Council on Artificial Intelligence, the Digital Charter Implementation Act, and the Global Partnership on AI. Canada also participates actively in international forums and standards-setting bodies to promote global alignment and interoperability on AI governance.

Human-centricity: Canada puts people at the center of its AI regulation. It aims to protect and promote human rights, dignity, and well-being in the design, development, and deployment of AI systems. Canada has adopted a set of ethical principles for responsible AI, which include human values, fairness, transparency, accountability, safety, and security. Canada also supports the development of human-centric AI applications that address social and environmental challenges, such as health equity, climate change, and gender equality.

Flexibility: Canada adopts a flexible and adaptive approach to AI regulation that balances innovation and protection. It recognizes that AI is a dynamic and evolving field that requires constant monitoring and evaluation. Canada does not impose a one-size-fits-all regulatory framework for AI, but rather tailors its oversight mechanisms according to the level of risk and impact of each AI system. Canada also encourages self-regulation and co-regulation by the AI industry through codes of conduct, best practices, certification schemes, and impact assessments.

Japan's AI Principles and Guidelines

Japan's AI governance framework is based on the Social Principles of Human-Centric AI (Social Principles), which were adopted by the Council for Integrated Innovation Strategy in March 2019. The Social Principles consist of 10 principles that aim to ensure that AI is used in a way that respects human dignity, human rights, and diversity. The 10 principles are:

- Principle of proper utilization
- Principle of human dignity and individual autonomy
- Principle of fairness
- Principle of transparency
- Principle of controllability
- Principle of safety
- Principle of security

- Principle of privacy
- Principle of accountability
- Principle of social harmony

The Social Principles are not legally binding, but rather serve as a common vision and value for AI development and utilization in Japan. They are intended to guide various stakeholders, such as AI system developers, operators, users, and regulators, in making ethical and responsible decisions regarding AI.

To operationalize the Social Principles, the Ministry of Economy, Trade and Industry (METI) established the Expert Group on Architecture for AI Principles to Be Practiced in 2019. The Expert Group published the AI Governance in Japan Ver. 1.1 in 2021, which provides an overview of Japan's AI governance structure and direction. The document also clarifies the trends and challenges of AI governance in Japan and abroad, and proposes some policy recommendations.

One of the key outcomes of the Expert Group is the Governance Guidelines for Implementation of AI Principles Ver. 1.1 (Guidelines), which were published in January 2022. The Guidelines provide practical guidance for AI system operators as well as developers on how to implement the Social Principles in their activities. The Guidelines cover various topics, such as risk assessment, stakeholder engagement, information disclosure, quality management, monitoring, auditing, and remediation.

The Guidelines adopt a risk-based approach to AI governance, which means that the level and type of governance measures should be proportional to the potential impact and likelihood of harm caused by AI systems. The Guidelines classify AI systems into three categories: low-risk systems that have no or negligible impact on human rights or social values; medium-risk systems that have moderate impact on human rights or social values; and high-risk systems that have significant impact on human rights or social values.

The Guidelines also adopt an agile approach to AI governance, which means that the governance measures should be flexible and adaptable to the changing environment and context of AI systems. The Guidelines emphasize the importance of continuous improvement and learning from feedback loops, as well as collaboration among multiple stakeholders, such as developers, operators, users, regulators, auditors, researchers, civil society organizations, and international organizations.

Japan's approach to AI regulation has significant implications for global AI governance. As one of the leading countries in developing and implementing AI principles and guidelines, Japan has contributed to shaping the international norms and standards for human-centric and responsible AI.

Japan has been actively involved in various international initiatives on AI governance, such as the G7/G20 Digital Ministers Meetings, the OECD

Recommendation on Artificial Intelligence, the UNESCO Recommendation on the Ethics of Artificial Intelligence, and the ISO/IEC JTC 1/SC 42 on Artificial Intelligence. Japan has also established bilateral dialogues on AI cooperation with countries such as France, Germany, the UK, the US, and India.

Japan's approach to AI regulation is also influential for other countries that are developing their own national frameworks for AI governance. Japan's approach provides a balanced and pragmatic model that respects human dignity and rights, while promoting innovation and competitiveness. Japan's approach also provides a collaborative and multistakeholder model that fosters dialogue and coordination among various actors involved in AI development and utilization.

Japan's approach to AI regulation is not without challenges and limitations, however. Japan still faces some issues, such as ensuring the consistency and coherence of AI regulations across different sectors and domains, enhancing the public awareness and literacy of AI, and addressing the social and economic impacts of AI, such as employment, education, and inclusion. Japan also needs to strengthen its engagement and leadership in the global arena, especially in addressing the emerging and complex challenges of AI, such as cross-border data flows, digital sovereignty, and human-machine interaction.

Japan's approach to AI regulation is not a final or perfect solution, but rather a dynamic and evolving one. Japan will continue to update and revise its AI governance framework in response to the changing environment and context of AI systems. Japan will also continue to share its experience and knowledge with other countries and stakeholders and contribute to the global dialogue and action on AI governance.

AI Regulations in Saudi Arabia and Middle East: Leading by Example

As artificial intelligence (AI) continues to evolve and integrate into various sectors, Saudi Arabia is taking proactive steps to regulate this powerful technology. The Kingdom recognizes the potential of AI to drive economic growth, enhance efficiency, and improve the quality of life for its citizens.

Saudi Arabia is pioneering the regulation of Artificial Intelligence (AI) in the Gulf Region with its proposed new Intellectual Property Law and the publication of AI Ethics Principles version 2.0 by the Saudi Data & Artificial Intelligence Authority (SDAIA). These developments are part of Saudi Arabia's vision to maximize data and AI's contribution to realizing the objectives of Vision 2030, aiming to contribute $135 billion to the GDP.

The draft new Intellectual Property Law of Saudi Arabia includes a chapter devoted to "Intellectual Property associated with Artificial Intelligence and Emerging Technologies and Supporting its Promotion". This chapter outlines that any IP created using AI technology will be protectable, with ownership attributed to the natural person who contributed to its creation. However, if the contribution of the natural person was insignificant or if the IP was generated by AI independently, then the IP will enter the public domain.

On September 14, 2023, SDAIA published their Artificial Intelligence Ethics Framework version 2.0. This framework is designed to help entities develop responsible AI-based solutions that limit negative implications while encouraging innovation. It applies to all entities that design, develop, deploy, implement, use, or are affected by AI systems in Saudi Arabia.

Saudi Arabia establishes the Seven Principles Governing AI Use and Development:

1. Fairness
2. Privacy and Security
3. Humanity
4. Social and Environmental Benefits
5. Reliability and Safety
6. Transparency and Explainability
7. Accountability and Responsibility

These principles are intended to guide entities through each stage of the AI System Lifecycle, ensuring that risk management is directly connected to AI initiatives.

Saudi Arabia's proactive approach in regulating AI demonstrates its commitment to fostering an environment where innovation thrives while ensuring ethical considerations are not overlooked. As AI continues to integrate into various sectors, such regulations will play a crucial role in shaping its future impact.

AI Initiatives Across the Middle East

Other Middle Eastern countries are also making significant strides in the AI domain. The United Arab Emirates (UAE), for example, appointed the world's first Minister for Artificial Intelligence in 2017, signaling its intent to be at the forefront of AI development and application. The UAE's National AI Strategy 2031 aims to position the country as a global leader in AI by 2031, focusing on sectors such as transport, health, space, renewable energy, water, technology, education, environment, and traffic.

In Qatar, the Qatar Computing Research Institute (QCRI) plays a pivotal role in advancing AI research and development, focusing on areas critical to national interest such as Arabic language technologies, social computing, and data analytics.

Regulatory Frameworks and Collaboration

The regulatory frameworks for AI in the Middle East are evolving, with a keen focus on fostering innovation while ensuring ethical standards. Saudi Arabia's and the UAE's strategies highlight a commitment to developing regulations that encourage AI adoption across industries while protecting citizens' rights and privacy.

Collaboration plays a crucial role in the development of AI in the region. Initiatives such as the AI for Good Global Summit and partnerships with global entities like the World Economic Forum (WEF) facilitate knowledge exchange and set benchmarks for AI ethics and governance.

Challenges and Future Directions

Despite these advances, the Middle East faces challenges, including the need for skilled AI talent and the alignment of AI regulations with rapid technological advancements. Addressing these challenges requires ongoing investment in education, research, and cross-border collaborations.

The future of AI in the Middle East is promising, with continued development of regulatory frameworks and strategic investments positioning the region as a global hub for AI innovation and ethical leadership.

AI Regulation in India: A Balancing Act

India is one of the fastest-growing economies in the world, with a large and talented pool of high-tech workers, a huge market potential, and a strong ambition to become a global leader in artificial intelligence (AI). AI technologies are already transforming various sectors in India, such as healthcare, education, agriculture, and smart cities, bringing benefits such as improved efficiency, quality, and accessibility. However, AI also poses significant challenges and risks, such as ethical dilemmas, social impacts, privacy violations, and security threats. How can India balance the opportunities and challenges of AI development and deployment? What are the current state and future perspectives of AI regulation in India?

The NITI Aayog is the apex public policy think tank of the Indian government, which has been tasked with establishing guidelines and policies for the development and use of AI in India. In 2018, the NITI Aayog released the National Strategy for Artificial Intelligence #AIForAll strategy, which featured AI research and development guidelines focused on five sectors: healthcare, agriculture, education, smart cities and infrastructure, and smart mobility and transportation. The strategy also identified some cross-cutting themes, such as data ecosystems, skilling and reskilling, ethics, privacy and security, collaboration and governance.

In 2021, the NITI Aayog released two approach papers on Principles for Responsible AI, which explored the various ethical considerations of deploying AI solutions in India. The first paper divided these considerations into system considerations and societal considerations. The system considerations mostly dealt with the overall principles behind decision-making, rightful inclusion of beneficiaries, and accountability of AI decisions. The societal considerations focused on the impact of automation on job creation and employment. The second paper focused on operationalizing principles for responsible AI. The report broke down the actions that need to be taken by both the government and the private sector, in partnership with research institutes, to cover regulatory and policy interventions, capacity building, incentivizing ethics by design, and creating frameworks for compliance with relevant AI standards.

In addition to the NITI Aayog's publications, the Indian government also enacted a new privacy law in 2023: the Digital Personal Data Protection Act. This law aims to protect the personal data of individuals from unauthorized collection, processing, storage, disclosure or misuse by data fiduciaries (entities that collect or process personal data). The law also establishes a Data Protection Authority to oversee and enforce compliance with the law. The law covers various aspects of data protection, such as consent, purpose limitation, data quality, data security, data breach notification, data localization, data portability, etc. The law also establishes a Data Protection Authority to oversee and enforce the law.

The challenges and opportunities for AI regulation in India faces several challenges and opportunities in developing and implementing a comprehensive and effective AI regulatory framework. Some of the key challenges include:

- Balancing innovation and regulation: India needs to strike a balance between promoting innovation and ensuring regulation of AI, without stifling creativity or compromising user rights. India needs to adopt a flexible and adaptive approach to AI regulation that can accommodate the rapid and dynamic changes in AI technologies and applications, while also addressing the emerging and evolving risks and challenges.
- Harmonizing national and international standards: India needs to align its national standards and policies with the international best practices

and norms for AI regulation, while also preserving its national interests and values. India needs to actively participate in the global dialogue and cooperation on AI governance, such as the GPAI, and contribute to the development of common principles, guidelines, and frameworks for responsible AI.

- Enhancing public awareness and participation: India needs to increase public awareness and understanding of AI, its benefits and risks, and its ethical and social implications. India also needs to foster public participation and engagement in the AI governance process, by soliciting feedback, inputs, and opinions from various stakeholders, such as users, consumers, civil society, academia, industry, etc.

- Building capacity and infrastructure: India needs to invest in building the capacity and infrastructure for AI development, adoption, and regulation. This includes enhancing the skills and competencies of the workforce, creating a robust data ecosystem, developing a secure and resilient digital infrastructure, establishing a strong research and innovation base, and creating a conducive legal and regulatory environment.

AI is a transformative technology that offers immense opportunities and challenges for India. The Indian government has adopted a balanced and pragmatic approach to AI regulation that aims to protect the rights and interests of users while enabling innovation and growth. However, there is still a lot of work to be done to develop and implement a comprehensive and effective AI regulatory framework that can address the complex and dynamic issues and risks posed by AI. India needs to overcome the challenges and seize the opportunities that AI presents and strive to achieve its vision of becoming a global AI hub that leverages AI for social good.

National Strategy for AI Development in Russia

In October 2019, President Vladimir Putin signed a decree approving the National Strategy for the Development of Artificial Intelligence over the period extending up to the year 2030. The strategy defines AI as "a set of technologies that enable machines to perform functions that are normally associated with human intelligence". The strategy sets out a number of short-term (to be completed by 2024) and medium-term (2030) qualitative goals designed to build Russia into a leading AI power.

The short-term goals include:

- Increasing the availability and quality of data for AI development and use
- Developing and implementing AI solutions for priority sectors, such as health care, education, agriculture, industry, public administration, defense, and security
- Creating a favorable environment for innovation and entrepreneurship in the field of AI
- Improving the personnel training system and increasing the number of specialists in AI
- Enhancing international cooperation and integration in the field of AI

The medium-term goals include:

- Achieving global leadership in the development and use of AI technologies
- Ensuring the widespread adoption of AI solutions in all sectors of society
- Increasing the competitiveness and efficiency of the national economy and social sphere through AI
- Improving the quality of life and well-being of citizens through AI
- Strengthening national security and sovereignty through AI

To achieve these goals, the strategy outlines a number of measures, such as:

- Establishing a national coordination center for AI development
- Creating digital platforms and infrastructure for data collection, processing, storage, and analysis
- Supporting research and development projects in the field of AI
- Providing financial and non-financial incentives for AI developers and users
- Developing standards and norms for AI quality, safety, and interoperability
- Developing ethical principles and guidelines for AI development and use
- Developing legal regulation for AI-related issues, such as liability, intellectual property rights, personal data protection, etc.
- Developing educational programs and courses for AI specialists and general public

- Promoting public awareness and engagement in the field of AI
- Participating in international forums and initiatives on AI governance

According to Federal Law No. 123-FZ, which came into force on July 1, 2020, Russia has introduced a special legal regime for "digital sandboxes" in Moscow. Digital sandboxes are territories where technologies may be developed and tested even if such technologies fall outside of the current legislation. The law also introduces definitions for artificial intelligence and artificial intelligence technology that may be used in future regulations.

The law allows companies to work on innovative AI technologies that are not regulated under existing legislation. It also creates opportunities for seeing how AI functions under real-life conditions. Additionally, the law is a first step in the legal regulation of AI in Russia since it introduces definitions for artificial intelligence and artificial intelligence technology that may be used in future regulations.

The duration of the experimental regime is five years. The experimental regime will also facilitate the realization of the Moscow government's project "Moscow - the Smart City 2030", which focuses on the development of smart living, smart mobility, smart economy, and smart environment in Russia's capital.

However, the law also raises some concerns regarding the protection of personal data involved in the experiments. For example, the law states that no personal data involved in the project can be transferred to persons not related to the experiment, nor can that data be stored outside of Moscow. This seems obscure, given the boundless nature of the Internet and the fact that cloud services are commonly used for data storage and access. Moreover, the personal data will still be at the disposal of the Moscow city government, as well as the entrepreneurs and legal entities entered into a special register of operators.

Another issue that needs to be addressed is the liability in cases of AI malfunction or fault. The law does not specify who is responsible for the damages or losses caused by AI systems or devices. This creates legal uncertainty and potential conflicts between the parties involved. Therefore, a clear and consistent legal framework for AI liability is needed to ensure accountability and trust in the field of AI.

Another challenge for AI regulation is to ensure that AI development and use are aligned with the ethical values and principles of society. Ethical regulation of AI aims to prevent or mitigate the negative impacts of AI on human dignity, rights, freedoms, and well-being. Ethical regulation of AI also aims to promote the positive impacts of AI on social good, justice, and human flourishing.

According to the National Strategy for AI Development, Russia plans to develop ethical principles and guidelines for AI development and use. The strategy states that "the development and use of artificial intelligence technologies must be based on respect for human dignity, rights, and freedoms, as well as on the principles of social justice, responsibility, transparency, security, and trust". The strategy also states that "the ethical regulation of artificial intelligence must take into account the cultural, historical, and religious traditions of the peoples of the Russian Federation".

However, the strategy does not provide any details on how these ethical principles and guidelines will be developed, implemented, or enforced. Moreover, the strategy does not address some of the key ethical issues that arise from AI development and use, such as:

- How to ensure that AI systems are fair, unbiased, and inclusive
- How to ensure that AI systems are transparent, explainable, and accountable
- How to ensure that AI systems respect human autonomy, privacy, and consent
- How to ensure that AI systems promote human values, interests, and preferences
- How to ensure that AI systems do not harm human dignity, rights, freedoms, or well-being

Therefore, a more comprehensive and participatory approach to ethical regulation of AI is needed to ensure that AI development and use are consistent with the moral values and expectations of society.

AI regulation in Russia is still in its early stages, but it shows some promising signs of progress and potential. The national strategy for AI development sets out ambitious goals and measures for building Russia into a leading AI power in the world. The legal regime for digital sandboxes creates opportunities for testing and experimenting with innovative AI technologies in Moscow. However, AI regulation in Russia also faces some significant challenges and risks, such as ensuring the protection of personal data, the liability for AI damages or losses, and the alignment of AI with ethical values and principles. Therefore, AI regulation in Russia requires more attention, dialogue, and collaboration among various stakeholders, such as government, industry, academia, civil society, and international partners.

Chapter 13: Generative AI Regulation

Generative AI is a branch of artificial intelligence that focuses on creating new content, such as images, text, music, or code, from existing data. Generative AI has many potential applications, such as enhancing creativity, improving education, and solving problems. However, generative AI also poses some challenges and risks, such as ethical, legal, and social implications. For example, generative AI can be used to create fake or misleading content, such as deepfakes, spam, or propaganda, which can harm individuals or society. Therefore, it is important to have regulations and guidelines for the development and use of generative AI.

Regulations for generative AI can help to ensure that the technology is used in a responsible and beneficial way, while respecting the rights and interests of all stakeholders. Regulations can also help to prevent or mitigate the negative impacts of generative AI, such as privacy violations, intellectual property infringements, or discrimination. Regulations can also foster trust and transparency among the users and developers of generative AI, as well as the public and policymakers.

However, regulating generative AI is not an easy task. There are many challenges and uncertainties involved, such as defining what constitutes generative AI, determining who is accountable for the outcomes of generative AI, and balancing innovation and protection. Moreover, generative AI is a fast-evolving and dynamic field, which requires constant monitoring and adaptation of the regulations. Therefore, regulating generative AI requires a collaborative and multidisciplinary approach involving various stakeholders from different sectors and backgrounds.

Some possible steps to implement effective regulations for generative AI are:

- Establishing a clear and consistent definition of generative AI and its scope
- Developing ethical principles and standards for the design and use of generative AI
- Creating legal frameworks and mechanisms for the governance and oversight of generative AI
- Providing education and awareness programs for the public and professionals on the benefits and risks of generative AI
- Encouraging research and innovation on the technical and social aspects of generative AI
- Promoting dialogue and cooperation among the stakeholders of generative AI at local, national, and international levels

Generative AI is a powerful and promising technology that can bring many opportunities and benefits to society. However, it also requires careful consideration and regulation to ensure that it is used in a safe and ethical manner. By working together, we can create a positive and sustainable future for generative AI.

Chapter 14: The Future of AI Governance

The future of AI governance is at the intersection of rapid technological advancements, evolving societal expectations, and the need for ethical oversight. This chapter explores emerging trends and technologies shaping the landscape of AI governance, anticipates potential scenarios and challenges in governing advanced AI systems, and proposes strategies for adapting and evolving AI governance frameworks over time.

Emerging Trends and Technologies

Quantum Computing

The advent of quantum computing presents both opportunities and challenges for AI governance. Quantum algorithms could revolutionize AI capabilities, but the increased computational power also raises concerns about the security and interpretability of AI systems. Future governance frameworks must grapple with the unique challenges posed by quantum-enhanced AI.

Autonomous Systems

Advancements in autonomous systems, including drones, vehicles, and robotic processes, necessitate specialized governance. The integration of AI into these systems raises questions about liability, safety, and ethical decision-making. Future AI governance frameworks must address the complexities of regulating autonomous technologies in various domains.

Explainable AI (XAI)

Explainable AI is gaining prominence as a response to the black-box nature of some advanced AI models. Future governance frameworks are likely to prioritize XAI to enhance transparency and accountability, ensuring that AI systems provide understandable explanations for their decisions, especially in critical applications such as healthcare and finance.

Potential Scenarios and Challenges

Superintelligent AI

The prospect of superintelligent AI introduces unprecedented challenges in governance. The development of AI systems surpassing human intelligence requires careful consideration of ethical and safety measures. Anticipating and addressing the risks associated with superintelligent AI is a crucial aspect of future governance frameworks.

Global Collaboration

As AI technologies transcend borders, achieving global collaboration on governance becomes increasingly complex. Differing cultural, legal, and ethical perspectives pose challenges in harmonizing international standards. Future governance must navigate these complexities while fostering cooperation to address shared challenges.

Adversarial AI

The rise of adversarial AI, where AI systems are manipulated to produce incorrect or harmful outcomes, poses a significant threat. Future governance frameworks need to incorporate robust security measures to defend against adversarial attacks, ensuring the integrity and reliability of AI systems.

Strategies for Adapting and Evolving

Continuous Research and Development

To stay ahead of technological advancements, governance frameworks must prioritize continuous research and development. Regular updates informed by the latest AI research will ensure that regulations remain relevant and effective in addressing emerging challenges.

Adaptive Regulatory Frameworks

Flexibility is key in the future of AI governance. Adaptive regulatory frameworks that can evolve in response to changing technologies and societal needs will be crucial. A dynamic approach allows for timely adjustments without compromising the overall integrity of governance structures.

Multi-Stakeholder Collaboration

Engaging a diverse set of stakeholders, including governments, industry, academia, and civil society, fosters a holistic approach to AI governance. Future frameworks should promote collaboration to ensure that regulations are informed by a broad range of perspectives and expertise.

Ethical AI Certification

The introduction of ethical AI certification could become a standard practice. This would involve independent third-party assessments to verify that AI systems adhere to ethical principles and governance standards. Certification can enhance transparency and build public trust in AI technologies.

Conclusion

The future of AI governance is shaped by the dynamic interplay of technological innovation, ethical considerations, and global collaboration. As emerging trends like quantum computing and autonomous systems redefine the AI landscape, governance frameworks must adapt to meet new challenges. Anticipating potential scenarios, addressing challenges such as superintelligent AI and adversarial attacks, and implementing strategies for continuous adaptation will be pivotal in shaping ethical, transparent, and effective AI governance for the future.

Chapter 15: Future of Global AI Regulation

The current state of AI regulations is diverse and fragmented. Different countries and regions have different approaches and priorities when it comes to regulating AI. The policymakers, researchers, industry leaders, civil society organizations, and citizens are grappling with several questions, challenges and impacts of AI as they seek to shape its future. In recent years, there has been a surge of initiatives and efforts to establish principles, guidelines, frameworks, and standards for ethical and trustworthy AI. Many countries and regions have also developed or proposed national or regional strategies and policies for AI governance. However, there is still a lack of global coordination and consensus on how to regulate AI in a harmonized and effective way.

Challenges and Opportunities for Global AI Regulation

One of the main challenges for global AI regulation is the diversity and complexity of AI applications and implications across different domains, sectors, contexts, and cultures. AI is not a monolithic or homogeneous phenomenon, but rather a multifaceted and dynamic one that evolves rapidly and continuously. Therefore, it is difficult to define, measure, and monitor AI in a comprehensive and consistent way. Moreover, different stakeholders may have different perspectives, interests, values, and expectations regarding AI development and use. Therefore, it is challenging to reconcile and align the various goals, priorities, norms, and standards that may exist or emerge at different levels of governance (local, national, regional, or global).

Another challenge for global AI regulation is the uncertainty and unpredictability of AI impacts and outcomes. AI is often characterized by opacity, complexity, autonomy, adaptability, and interactivity, which make it hard to understand, explain, control, or anticipate its behavior and effects. Furthermore, AI may interact with other complex systems (such as human or natural systems) in nonlinear and emergent ways that may generate unintended or unforeseen consequences. Therefore, it is difficult to assess and mitigate the potential risks and harms that may arise from AI use or misuse. Moreover, it is difficult to establish and enforce accountability and responsibility for AI actions or decisions.

A third challenge for global AI regulation is the asymmetry and inequality of AI development and access. There is a significant gap between the leading countries or regions that have advanced capabilities and resources for AI research and innovation (such as the US, China, or the EU) and the developing countries or regions that lack such capacities or opportunities (such as Africa or Latin America). This gap may create or exacerbate power imbalances and dependencies in the global AI ecosystem. Furthermore, there is a significant disparity between the privileged groups or individuals that have access to or benefit from AI products or services (such as wealthy or educated people) and the marginalized groups or individuals that are excluded from or harmed by AI applications or implications (such as poor or vulnerable people). This disparity may create or worsen social injustices and inequalities in global society.

Despite these challenges, there are also opportunities for global AI regulation. One opportunity is the potential for positive social impact and value creation. AI can offer solutions and benefits for many pressing global issues and needs such as poverty alleviation, climate change mitigation healthcare improvement education enhancement and human rights protection AI can also enable new forms of creativity Collaboration and participation for human empowerment and well-being Therefore it is important to promote and support the development and deployment of ethical and beneficial AI that can serve the common good and public interest.

Another opportunity for global AI regulation is the possibility for mutual learning and exchange. AI can facilitate knowledge sharing and information dissemination across different domains sectors contexts and cultures. AI can also foster dialogue and communication among different stakeholders with diverse perspectives, interests' values, and expectations. Therefore, it is important to encourage and enable the participation and engagement of all relevant actors in the co-creation and co-governance of AI that can reflect the diversity and complexity of human society.

A third opportunity for global AI regulation is the availability of existing and emerging platforms and mechanisms for international cooperation and dialogue on AI issues. There are many initiatives and efforts that aim to provide guidance or support for AI governance at the global level, such as the OECD Principles on AI, the UNESCO Recommendation on the Ethics of AI, the UN Secretary-General's Roadmap for Digital Cooperation, the Global

Partnership on AI, the IEEE Global Initiative on Ethics of Autonomous and Intelligent Systems, and the World Economic Forum's Centre for the Fourth Industrial Revolution. These platforms and mechanisms can offer opportunities for coordination, collaboration, and convergence among different actors and stakeholders on common goals, priorities, norms, and standards for AI regulation.

The future of AI regulations is uncertain and dynamic. As AI evolves and becomes more pervasive and impactful, new challenges and opportunities will emerge that will require new or updated regulations. Moreover, as different actors and stakeholders interact and influence each other in the global AI ecosystem, there will be a need for more coordination and cooperation to harmonize AI regulations across borders and domains.

Conclusion: Balance Between Innovation, AI Governance and AI Regulations

Artificial intelligence (AI) is transforming the world in unprecedented ways. From healthcare to education, from entertainment to transportation, AI is enabling new possibilities and solutions for humanity. However, AI also poses significant challenges and risks, such as ethical dilemmas, social impacts, legal uncertainties, and security threats. How can we ensure that AI is developed and deployed in a responsible and beneficial manner? How can we balance the need for innovation and the need for governance and regulation of AI?

One possible answer is to adopt a human-centric approach to AI, which puts the values and rights of human beings at the core of AI design and use. This means that AI should respect human dignity, autonomy, privacy, and diversity, and that it should promote human well-being, justice, and democracy. A human-centric approach also implies that humans should have the ability to understand, control, and oversee AI systems, and that they should be accountable for their actions and decisions involving AI.

A human-centric approach to AI requires a multi-stakeholder collaboration among various actors, such as governments, businesses, researchers, civil society, and users. These actors should work together to establish common principles, standards, and norms for AI, as well as to implement effective mechanisms for oversight, transparency, and accountability. Moreover, these actors should engage in an open and inclusive dialogue with each other and with the public to foster trust, awareness, and participation in AI-related matters.

A human-centric approach to AI also demands a continuous and adaptive learning process, which recognizes the dynamic and evolving nature of AI and its impacts. This means that AI governance and regulation should be flexible and responsive to new developments and challenges, as well as to the diversity of contexts and applications of AI. Furthermore, this means that AI governance and regulation should be based on evidence and data, as well as on ethical and social considerations.

In conclusion, balancing innovation and governance of AI is not an easy task, but it is a necessary one. By adopting a human-centric approach to AI, we can harness the potential of AI for good while mitigating its risks for harm. We can also ensure that AI serves the interests of humanity rather than the other way around.

Appendices

Appendix 1: Bibliography

- IBM: AI Governance - What is AI governance? | IBM
- OECD AI Principles - AI-Principles Overview - OECD.AI

- Hafiz Sheikh Adnan Ahmed, C., CDPSE, GDPR-CDPO (2022). "Developing an Artificial Intelligence Governance Framework." from https://www.isaca.org/resources/news-and-trends/newsletters/atisaca/2022/volume-38/developing-an-artificial-intelligence-governance-framework.

- . "AI governance: Ensuring your AI is transparent, compliant, and trustworthy." from https://www.ibm.com/analytics/common/smartpapers/ai-governance-smartpaper/.

- FRANKE, U. (2021). "Artificial Intelligence diplomacy - Artificial Intelligencegovernance as a new European Union external policy tool." PE 662.926 – June 2021.

- (2023)"AI diplomacy." from https://www.diplomacy.edu/topics/ai-and-diplomacy/.

- (2023). Executive Order on the Safe, Secure, and Trustworthy Development and Use of Artificial Intelligence. U. Governament, White House. **14110**.

- Council of Europe: <u>Artificial Intelligence and Human Rights - Commissioner for Human Rights (coe.int)</u>

- UNESCO Recommendation on the Ethics of AI: <u>AI governance and human rights | Chatham House – International Affairs Think Tank</u>

- Accountability in AI: <u>Accountability in artificial intelligence: what it is and how it works | AI & SOCIETY (springer.com)</u>

- Harvard Business Review: <u>Building Transparency into AI Projects (hbr.org)</u>

- Office of Privacy Commissioner of Canada: <u>Office of the Privacy Commissioner of Canada - Office of the Privacy Commissioner of Canada</u>

- (2016). General Data Protection Regulation. E. P. A. O. T. COUNCIL, European Union. **2016/679:** 88.

- . "AI diplomacy." from <u>https://www.diplomacy.edu/topics/ai-and-diplomacy/</u>.

- Artificial Intelligence ICO UK, <u>Website under maintenance | ICO</u>

- AI Auditing Framework, UCO Uk, <u>Website under maintenance | ICO</u>

- Decree of the President of the Russian Federation on the Development of Artificial Intelligence in the Russian Federation. <u>http://publication.pravo.gov.ru/Document/View/0001201910110003</u>

- Federal Law No. 123-FZ on Introducing Amendments into Certain Legislative Acts of the Russian Federation Regarding Experimental Legal

Regimes in Order to Ensure Technological Development in Moscow.

http://publication.pravo.gov.ru/Document/View/0001202007010001

- "Saudi Arabia's National Strategy for Data & AI." SDAIA.

- "Arab AI Summit." Arab AI Organization.

- "Saudi Arabia's Vision 2030 and Artificial Intelligence: An Assessment" - Journal of Middle Eastern Politics and Policy

- UAE Government. "National Artificial Intelligence Strategy 2031."

- Qatar Computing Research Institute (QCRI).

Appendix 2: Abbreviations in the Book

AG: Artificial Intelligence Governance

AI: Artificial Intelligence

AIA: Artificial Intelligence Act

CV: Computer Vision

EO: Executive Order

EU: European Union

FTC: Federal Trade Commission

GDPR: General Data Protection Regulation

GenAI: Generative Artificial Intelligence

ICO: Information Commissioner's Office in the United Kingdom

ML: Machine Learning

NLP: Natural Language Processing

OECD: Organization for Economic Co-operation and Development

OPC: Office of the Privacy Commissioner

PIPEDA: Personal Information Protection and Electronic Documents Act

UNESCO: United Nations Educational, Scientific and Cultural Organization

Acknowledgements

I would like to express my heartfelt gratitude to everyone who contributed to the completion of this book. Writing a book is a collaborative effort, and I am fortunate to have had the support and encouragement of many incredible individuals.

First and foremost, I extend my deepest appreciation to my family, whose unwavering encouragement and support made it possible for me to dedicate the necessary time and energy to this project. Your encouragement has been my source of strength.

I am indebted to my friends and colleagues for their valuable insights, thoughtful feedback, and constant encouragement throughout the writing process. Your diverse perspectives enriched the content and helped shape the final manuscript.

Special thanks to Tony Rook, and Anoop Aggarwal for their inputs, meticulous attention to detail, constructive feedback, and dedication to refining the manuscript. Their expertise played a crucial role in bringing this book to its best possible form. Thank you to Nancy Hadley for writing the foreword and being a positive influence in my life.

Lastly, I want to express my gratitude to all the readers who embark on this journey with me. Your interest and engagement in the ideas presented in this book are the ultimate reward.

Thank you to everyone who played a part in making this book a reality. Your contributions have not gone unnoticed, and I am truly thankful for your presence in this literary journey.

About the Author

Ira Goel is an experienced CISO and DPO who has a consulting company offering risk management, AI governance, and data protection services. Ira writes blogs, white papers and articles on several well-known organizations to share her knowledge and learnings from her professional experience.

Born and raised in India, Ira developed a passion for connecting the dots and finding at an early age, drawing inspiration from her diverse cultural background and life experiences. Ira holds two master's degrees from India and the Unites States, and is pursuing a third Master's degree from University of Maastricht in the Netherlands. Ira's academic background, coupled with a natural curiosity, has driven her to explore various facets of Artificial Intelligence, providing readers with a fresh and nuanced take on the subject.

With a keen interest in learning and sharing, Ira brings a unique blend of simplicity and expression to her work. Her commitment to Artificial Intelligence and AI Governance is evident on every page, offering readers a thoughtfully crafted journey through the complexities of AI.

"I believe in the power of simplifying complex topics to bridge gaps, foster understanding, and inspire change" says Ira. Her debut book, Introduction to AI, AI Governance and AI Regulations, reflects this belief, inviting readers to explore AI in a way that is both enlightening and emotionally resonant.

When she's not immersed in the world of trends and patterns, Ira enjoys driving, gardening and photography. She has diverse hobbies and enjoys her time exploring opportunities in life.

Connect with Ira on LinkedIn or visit her website to stay updated on her latest projects and musings.

Visit the website

Connect on LinkedIn